"In *Holding the Rope*, Ryan Martin prov
Scripture and toward healthy sending and
sending missionaries, Martin challenges u
nership with our sent ones. Missions pasto
aries would do well to pick up this simple

Matthew Bennett, Assistant Professor of Missions and Theology, Cedarville University

"This biblically rooted, thought-provoking work helps us understand our mandate to continue participating in God's mission. The sending church is critical to the ongoing process of global gospel proclamation. This is a resource I will recommend time and time again to churches that are serious about the Great Commission and taking their place in God's plan. Every church staff member and missions advocate needs to read this book."

Sandy Wisdom-Martin, Executive Director-Treasurer, Woman's Missionary Union

"The Protestant Missionary Movement has a long history that has resulted in the Church learning a great deal about communication, culture, and context. However, when it comes to missionary care, we still have much to learn. Ryan Martin has done a great job reminding us that whenever churches send people to the nations, relationships are not ending; rather, new partnerships—with new responsibilities—are beginning. *Holding the Rope* is a most helpful resource that assists churches in understanding the why, what, and how of missionary care. Looking for a book to lead your church in the proper direction? Here it is!"

J. D. Payne, missiologist, Professor of Christian Ministry, Samford University

"*Holding the Rope* is an excellent resource for sending churches, agencies, and sent ones as they consider their ongoing role and responsibilities to one another in mission. It contains very practical ideas for strengthening and supporting missionaries to ensure ministry longevity and fruitfulness throughout their careers. A must-read for missionary sending and supporting churches!"

Steven M. Ellis, Executive Pastor for Church Planting & Missions, First Baptist Rogers, Arkansas (Former Affinity Group Leader, East Asia, International Mission Board)

"In 1793, William Carey, who would later become known as the Father of Modern Missions, gave us the famous rope-holder imagery this book champions. Carey was willing to go down into India's 'goldmine of souls,' but his willingness came with a caveat: 'You must hold the ropes.' Over 200 years later, the ropes that once hoisted missionaries and supported kingdom advancement have been severed, tugged back upward, and largely abandoned. As a result, we require a new strategy to tether Church resources and Christian relationships to global kingdom workers serving around the world. Thankfully, in this pivotal moment, Ryan Martin's *Holding the Rope* promises to do just that. Read on! You'll be inspired to help create global impact by joining God's glorious mission mandate."

David Joannes, Founder/CEO of Within Reach Global, author of *The Mind of a Missionary*

"As Christian leaders, we talk a lot about missions and reaching the least-reached. That's a good thing! Sadly, however, the excitement of commissioning one to be sent often ends soon after they arrive on the field. Ryan Martin gives us a different playbook, one that encourages us to send the very best from our church and to be intentional in our sending before they get to the field, while they are on the field, and even when they return after finishing their ministry service. He takes us from the first moment to the last moment of the sending process in this very practical book. If you are a church leader, one who has been sent, or you know someone who has been sent, read this book, and then keep it for reference and consult it often. I've been waiting for a book like this, and I trust you will be greatly helped by this resource."

Dave Furman, Senior Pastor, Redeemer Church of Dubai, author of *Being There* and *Kiss the Wave*

Holding the Rope:

HOW THE LOCAL CHURCH CAN CARE FOR ITS SENT ONES

Holding the Rope:

HOW THE LOCAL CHURCH CAN CARE FOR ITS SENT ONES

Ryan Martin

UPSTREAM
COLLECTIVE

Permissions, The Upstream Collective,
P.O. Box 23871
Knoxville, TN 37933.

www.theupstreamcollective.org

ISBN: 978-1-7343705-8-4

Printed in the United States of America

Unless otherwise indicated, all Scripture quotations are from the Holy Bible, English Standard Version® (ESV®), copyright © 2001 by Crossway, a publishing ministry of Good News Publishers. Used by permission. All rights reserved.

Editor: David McWhite

Cover and Interior design: Hayley Moss, Moss Photo and Design, LLC
hayleyrmoss@gmail.com

In loving memory of my grandmother, Margaret Martin—

Thank you for being a faithful rope-holder for members of your local church, for countless missionaries sent out through the IMB, for the Women's Missionary Union (WMU) through your decades of service, and, most notably, for me. I recall your keen interest in every missions opportunity in which I endeavored, your excitement to hear of the doors of opportunity the Lord had opened, and the impact your labor in prayer had and continues to have on me—in marriage, through ministry, and on mission.

May there be many more in the local church to hold the rope tightly as you did.

We recall, in the presence of our God and Father, your work produced by faith, your labor motivated by love, and your endurance inspired by hope in our Lord Jesus Christ.

— 1 Thessalonians 1:3

TABLE OF CONTENTS

After the team from our local church left to return to the United States, my wife and I were a mix of emotions. Over the next few days, however, one emotion rose to the top—thankfulness. Not only had the team ministered to us, but they had also invested in our work and ministry location. As we talked with a few fellow sent ones in the area, they were amazed that an entire team, including the pastor, had come simply to care for us and spend some time ministering alongside us for a few days. One family, who had served on the field for over a decade, mentioned that they had never had any church leadership visit them. My wife and I were grateful that we were part of a local church that took the sending and missionary care of its sent ones seriously.

Ryan Martin is correct when he states, "Partnership between the sent one and the sending church encourages missionary retention, thus helping facilitate the spread of the gospel." I am convinced that one of the deficiencies among local churches is in our ongoing care for our sent ones. This deficiency hurts the health of our missionaries and hampers the longevity of their gospel witness.

Our churches are all fans of the Great Commission. We love making a big deal of sending out men, women, and families to the mission field during a commissioning service, and spending a few minutes on Sunday morning praying for those we have sent is a highlight in many of our churches. But the healthy sending of men, women, and families as cross-cultural missionaries does not begin and end with a commissioning service and requires more than briefly highlighting them during prayer. Faithful sending is a commitment to the ongoing opportunity and responsibility to care for those we send. Caring well for our sent ones moves us from fandom to fuller participation in the Great Commission.

Consider the reunion of Paul and Barnabas to their sending church of Antioch toward the end of Acts 14:

". . . they sailed back to Antioch where they had been commended to the grace of God for the work they had now completed. After they arrived and gathered the church together, they reported everything God had done with them . . ." (vv. 26–27)

The church at Antioch sent out and then gladly received Paul and Barnabas. When these sent ones arrived back at Antioch, the Scriptures recount that they reported all that God had done with them. In other words, Paul and Barnabas were able to celebrate and process the amazingly good things God did as well as the incredibly difficult things they experienced along the way (read chapters 13 and 14 for the rest of the story). In a similar way, our sent ones come back home with a combination of the highlights of life and ministry and the wounds and scars from the battle.

The last verse in Acts 14 says that Paul and Barnabas "spent a considerable time" with the disciples (v. 28). This reconnection and celebration with their sending church did not end with one report. There was a considerable investment of time and resources in Paul and Barnabas. The church at Antioch was faithful in sending and faithful in caring well for their sent ones. Your sent ones need churches committed to sending them well and to gladly receiving them back as you walk with them through the good and bad of their missionary experience.

As more and more churches are convinced of their personal role in God's mission among the nations, many are now grappling with what it means to care for their sent ones. I, for one, am thankful. There's that emotion again.

The book you have in your hands holds the next step in your commitment to healthy sending. In *Holding the Rope*, Martin gives a hopeful framework for thinking well and implementing a system of caring for sent ones that recognizes the church's unique roles and responsibilities in the process. Whether you are on the front end of creating a missionary care system or simply trying to strengthen how you care, this book will walk you through each step along the way. Further, you will answer some practical questions and discover field-tested ideas for how your church can better care for its sent ones.

Holding the Rope provides the tools to build a robust missionary care framework for your local church or missions agency, and my hope is that long-term commitment to caring for our sent ones becomes the normative pattern in the years ahead for church and agency alike. As you read through this book, let it encourage you toward prioritizing care for those you help send. As all of us commit to care in more profound ways for our sent ones, I believe it will enhance our celebration of all that God is doing through them among all peoples and places.

My prayer is that this book will lead you and your church into a new season of sending and caring well for those you send. Churches must keep sending missionaries and commit to sending in a healthy way. Churches who are committed to healthy sending will care well for their sent ones, and in caring well for your sent ones, God is glorified, gospel witness is strengthened, and your missionaries will be—you guessed it—thankful.

Greg Mathias
New Orleans Baptist Theological Seminary
Lakeshore Church
New Orleans, LA

ACKNOWLEDGEMENTS

This project would not have happened without others holding the rope for me as I endeavored to research and write this resource for the sender and the sent one.

The love, support, prayers, and service of my wife, Rebekah, throughout this project were a rich blessing. I am grateful to partner alongside her as we raise our children to know, love, and follow the Lord, wherever he may send them. I pray the Lord would empower us to glorify him with one voice among our neighbors and throughout the nations.

My children, Hudson Isaiah, Annie Rose, and Hattie Jane, have been a constant source of encouragement, love, and joy throughout this process. I pray that the Lord would continue to grow their knowledge and love for Christ, his church, his Word, and his world, and that he might save and use them each to send and support to the ends of the earth.

My parents, Ken and Pam Martin, are a model of constant rope-holders for our family, whether in marriage, ministry, or missions. They always encourage me along the way to keep learning and writing for King Jesus.

Dr. Greg Mathias, Larry McCrary, Bradley Bell, David McWhite, and the team at Upstream Collective and Upstream Sending were a steady support and guide. Their Great Commission heartbeat is evidenced throughout this book. They each, in their own ways, have pushed me to be a better writer, student of the Scriptures, minister of the gospel, and mobilizer to the nations. They have helped make this project, I pray, a valuable tool to equip churches to send well.

Lightbearers Ministries, the local church I served previously, and the one I am a member of currently provided me with the resources, the time, and the encouragement to labor in this work and have empowered me to model, in ministry service, the raising up and supporting of missionaries. I pray this project serves churches and ministries like theirs, and others, and results in greater gospel partnerships between sent ones, sending churches, and mission agencies.

The missionaries highlighted in this work and others I have partnered with and continue to partner alongside are worthy examples of service that is bold yet humble, convictional yet compassionate, faithful and sacrificial as they continue to declarate and demonstrate his glorious gospel among the nations. I appreciate their transparency in sharing how churches and agencies can partner more effectively to see them thrive on the field. Thank you for abandoning it all for the sake of the call. May we, as senders, keep holding the rope tightly for you.

Jay Decker, Jaime Haguewood, and Ron and Lisa Jones demonstrated their eager desire to partner with the local church in caring for sent ones. Bradley Bell, Matt Clark, and Scott Ward are to be thanked for the ways they and the churches they pastor model faithful sending and supporting.

Finally, I praise Jesus for calling me to himself and commissioning me to go to the ends of the earth and support others who go forth for the sake of the Name. This book is for the advancement of his gospel, the building of his church, the support of his ambassadors, and the praise of his glory among every tribe, tongue, and nation.

INTRODUCTION

Churches may see their role in sending members to the ends of the earth as the finish line instead of the beginning of a partnership. Some churches even lose their identity as the lead role in the sending process along the way. Steve Beirn, author of Well Sent, affirms, "The local church has not remained at the center of sending. Often, the individual considering global ministry is at the center of the process, partly due to the fact that the church has not assumed ownership."[1] He notes that agencies often end up being the ones in charge of the sending process. In his book Mind the Gaps: Engaging Your Church in Member Care, missions pastor and author David Wilsons highlights that mission agencies have a role to play, but that "the church is uniquely equipped to minister to its missionaries, especially when it sees gaps in care that the agencies, for whatever reason, do not or cannot provide . . . it would be completely negligent to simply delegate or outsource the responsibility of missionary care completely to agencies."[2] Wilson describes the investment churches provide as giving birth, nurturing, and equipping its members to serve on the field. They have a unique role and responsibility to care for those with whom they already have a mutual relationship.[3] The church should take ownership in the supporting and sustaining care for missionaries, even when those missionaries are in partnership with a mission agency.

So why is member care so important that I would set out to write a book to resource the church in caring well for her sent ones? First, I believe faithfulness to the task of the Great Commission is in direct correlation to our faithfulness to send and support well. Studies show that the average length of stay for a missionary on the field is two to four years, with close to half of missionaries leaving the field within their first five years. While those statis-

---

1 Steve Beirn and George W. Murray, *Well Sent: Reimagining the Church's Missionary-Sending Process* (Fort Washington, PA: CLC Publications, 2015), 20.

2 David J. Wilson, ed., *Mind the Gaps: Engaging the Church in Missionary Care* (Colorado Springs, CO: Believers, 2015), 5–6.

3 Ibid., 6–7.

tics are staggering, the greater concern is that over 70 percent of the reasons given for a swift exit were preventable.[4] If churches begin caring for their missionaries long before they commission them, then they can better stabilize, support, and strengthen their sent ones' faithfulness to the task.

Second, the Scriptures speak to the local church's responsibility in setting apart, sending, and supporting missionaries. We will unpack three texts that reveal the church is to support generously, give of its time, finances, and people sacrificially, and partner responsibly. Because the church is the primary means through which the Great Commission is carried out, the care of the church's sent ones should not be outsourced solely to a missions agency (although I will argue that the agency has a role to play in providing care).

A third reason for putting this resource together is my personal passion for missionary care. Prior to my current role in missions mobilization, I served for thirteen years as a local church missions pastor. When members would ask what I loved about my position, I would often state that I appreciated having one foot in the church and one foot on the field. I am administratively gifted, which has served me well in missions mobilization and equipping; however, what greatly energizes me is being with sent ones on the field— breathing their air, walking their streets, eating their food, and hearing their victories, heartaches, challenges, concerns, and hopes within cross-cultural ministry. I have known the reality of meeting with missionaries whose children didn't acclimate well to the field, praying against the enemy's attacks, and asking the Holy Spirit to give them the sustaining grace and power they needed. I have counseled a family who had reached the point of burnout as they transitioned from a village setting to urban life and were having to learn a different pace of work and rest. Still other opportunities have come my way, like refueling long-term workers by sending them short-term assistance and support. Being able to pray with, encourage, and exhort missionaries with the Word through calls, emails, and field visits is a great joy and delight that not only the missions pastor can take part in, but that the entire church can experience as well.

Through my studies on this issue, I saw the need for sending churches to provide faithful missionary care for their sent ones, and I began to think through how I could help them understand their role in missionary care and

4 ReMAP and ReMAP II are some of the most thorough mission research studies conducted just before and shortly after the turn of the millennium with regard to missionary retention. ReMAP is an acronym for Reducing Missionary Attrition Project. The research contained in them was conducted by the Mission Commission of the World Evangelical Alliance. The fieldwork in ReMAP II involved 600 agencies across 22 countries and represents some 40,000 missionaries. The effort was primarily led by William D. Taylor. World Evangelical Alliance, "ReMAP II: Worldwide Missionary Retention Study & Best Practices," 10, http://www.worldevangelicals.org/ resources/rfiles/res3_96_link_1292358945.pdf.

develop a strategy for providing that care. I began by working from a biblical foundation and an understanding of historical and contemporary examples of missionary care. In addition, I sought insight from the mission field, mission agencies, and local churches on best practices and gaps in missionary care today. Many of the voices you'll hear testimony from are missionaries on the field whom I have personally interacted with as one of their pastors. Certainly, I and others in the church didn't do everything perfectly, but we sought to be faithful in sending and supporting well. I long for local churches to take up the responsibility and joy that I have experienced having one foot in the church and one foot on the field. Many churches, though, need an understanding of both the why and the how of missionary care, and that is what I aim for this resource to provide. In the book that follows, I have sought to provide a biblical and practical foundation for providing missionary care in the pre-field, on-field, and post-field stages. My hope in offering the content that follows is that it will inspire churches to step up for the sake of their missionaries and step into their God-given role as missionary care providers.

In his article "Don't Just Be a Sending Church, Be a Staying Church," Aaron Menikoff writes,

> It's not enough to be a sending church. You need to be a staying church. A staying church doesn't let the rope fray or the bond loosen. As inconvenient as the relationship may be, the staying church remains involved by praying faithfully, communicating regularly, visiting occasionally, and always looking for new and creative ways to help. This is how we hold the rope, and we mustn't let go.[5]

Churches that send and support well in partnership with a mission agency will develop long-lasting relationships with their sent ones that help sustain field personnel, promote the furtherance of the gospel and the church, and result in the glory of God.

---

5 Aaron Menikoff, "Don't Just Be a Sending Church, Be a Staying Church," *Reaching & Teaching Blog*, 24 November 2020, https://rtim.org/dont-just-be-a-sending-church-be-a-staying-church/.

SECTION ONE

Biblical and Theological Foundations of Missionary Care

A strong partnership between the sent one and the sending church encourages missionary retention, thus helping facilitate the spread of the gospel. To gain insight into how churches can best care for those they commission and send to the mission field, we can look to certain passages of Scripture to help discern biblical principles to apply toward a strategy for missionary care. While numerous biblical examples provide insight, three passages give particular focus to caring for sent ones: 3 John 5–8, Philippians 2:25–30, and Acts 14:26–28.

CHAPTER 1

Missionary Care in 3 John 5–8

Beloved, it is a faithful thing you do in all your efforts for these brothers, strangers as they are, who testified to your love before the church. You will do well to send them on their journey in a manner worthy of God. For they have gone out for the sake of the name, accepting nothing from the Gentiles. Therefore we ought to support people like these, that we may be fellow workers for the truth.

Missionary care should begin early in the stages of pre-field assessment, training, and equipping. Bonds that can withstand the ups and downs of life on the field develop when relationships form with missionaries before they reach the mission field. Knowledge gained by the local church in pre-field assessment and experience helps foster the development of the physical, emotional, mental, and spiritual well-being of a missionary before they cross into a new culture.

Church leaders should recruit like coaches. Successful coaches know what type of players they want, and instead of waiting for them to surface, they seek them out. These coaches find players who want to be on the team and who are eager to do the work required to be successful. I recall coming back from a vision trip to East Asia where we discovered an opportunity to use football as a pathway for gospel proclamation. Immediately, my teammate and I knew exactly who would be well-suited to lead this ministry. Just like a coach, I approached these two individuals, who both had a heart for the nations and a passion for football, and presented the opportunity. They prayed and answered the call to go, and they ended up spending more than six months serving alongside long-term workers, having many fruitful gospel conversations, and supporting the long-term work of church planting. By being proactive rather than reactive, we gave these young men a chance to see their God-given gifts, talents, and desires come together for missionary service.

Leaders within churches ought to take the same approach when considering the task of equipping and releasing members to the mission field. Mack Stiles, missionary to the Middle East, says, "Healthy churches produce healthy Christians who become healthy missionaries."[6] The local church, both its members and leaders, should be sending and supporting well for the promotion and advancement of the gospel. We see in 3 John 5–8 how missionary care happens in the sending of missionaries, primarily through local churches, for the sake of the gospel. John's exhortation in this passage demonstrates the centrality of local churches in the care and support of sent ones.

Background

Understanding the background of this letter will help us see why John used his third epistle to encourage missionary support by the local church. A quick survey of the Gospel of John and John's letters shows a very close relationship between all four writings. The Gospel of John focuses on the ministry of Jesus, and just as Jesus experienced conflict with his Jewish contemporaries, so too would such conflict arise for John's hearers. Colin Kruse explains that, after the writing of John's Gospel, certain members within this larger community of John's readers adopted beliefs denying the person and work of Jesus. This group, called secessionists, eventually split off and proclaimed heresy and caused confusion within the church.[7] John wrote his first epistle to bolster believers in their faith in Jesus and in what he had accomplished through the cross. Second John warns of false itinerant preachers. John uses this third letter to encourage Gaius and the church to support and send laborers to the harvest field to promote the gospel. Kruse emphasizes, "The 'brothers' who had been recipients of Gaius' hospitality were most likely members of the elder's community and reported to it and regarded his community as their base. They had gone out as itinerant preachers, and, following the pattern laid down by Jesus (Matt 10:10–11), they depended on the hospitality of Gaius in the places they visited."[8] John set apart his friend who he found faithful in this task and identified the church as the conduit through which the gospel advances.

Exegetical Context

Gaius sent and faithfully supported missionaries, making his example

6 Mack Stiles, "9 Marks of Healthy Missions," *9 Marks Journal: Missions* (Fall 2015), 31.
7 Colin G. Kruse, *The Letters of John*, PNTC (Grand Rapids: Eerdmans, 2000), 2.
8 Ibid., 43.

one worth studying. John uses the word "beloved" to refer to Gaius in verses 1 and 5. Robert Yarbrough writes that "the use of beloved shows that John and Gaius enjoyed a warm relationship that was mutually bound together in Christian love (3 John 1, 5) and truth (3 John 1, 3, 4, 8, 12), and expressed in an understanding and love for the local church."[9] Danny Akin argues that "Gaius would treat strangers in this faithful manner [giving] further testimony of the fact that he was walking in the truth."[10] Gaius' speech and actions spoke the same message. He not only helped meet their needs but facilitated a communal bond as well. Kruse points out that "such hospitality involved more than just food and sleep but welcoming them into that community as one of their own."[11] Gaius was commended for both the quantity and quality of hospitality he extended. He modeled how local church members, because they are bound in Christian love and truth, should be marked by hospitality toward those they support.

Hospitality is a unique characteristic of missionary care. In the same manner that this church in 3 John received missionaries into their fold, I recall us welcoming into membership two missionaries who had ties to the church (one even had family members in our church), but who weren't members themselves. As our sending church relationship with them grew, a strong personal relationship began to develop, and these families eventually joined our church while on stateside assignment. Before they returned to the field, we recommissioned them and committed to a long-term partnership through which we provided ongoing care.

Individuals and churches in the first century exemplified such hospitality in how they received strangers and traveling missionaries who then reported back to their own community. John received such a report about Gaius and writes that these guests "testified to your love before the church" (v.6).[12] Yarbrough writes, "Part of the fabric of fellowship in the gospel is coworkers (in this case Gaius) stepping up and executing so that ministry opportunities are met and others (in this case John) are gratified and encouraged."[13] Gaius graciously received these missionaries, and now John writes that he must "send them on their journey in a manner worthy of God" (v. 6). John Stott argues that "sending them on their way" meant supporting these missionaries on their next journey.[14] The writer gives an admonition not only to send

---

9 Robert W. Yarbrough, 1–3 John, BECNT 15 (Grand Rapids: Baker Academic, 2008), 363.

10 Daniel Akin, 1, 2, 3 John, NAC 38 (Nashville: Holman Reference, 2001), 242–43.

11 Kruse, 222.

12 The word for "church" (ekklesia) used here and two other times in the book (vv.9, 10) refers to the local church.

13 Yarbrough, 372.

14 John R. W. Stott, The Letter of John, TNTC 19 (Downers Grove: InterVarsity Press Academic, 1988), 229.

missionaries, but to do so "in a manner worthy of God." Glenn Barker illustrates that these brothers were recognized as servants of God, and "in such instances, Christians were to provide hospitality as if the Lord himself were being welcomed (cf. John 13:20, Gal 4:14–15 and Heb 13:2)."[15] Churches today should strive to be known as those who welcome well in this way.

What was the purpose for sending out these brothers? Verse 7 explains that they went out "for the sake of the Name." This phrase occurs four times in the book of Acts (5:41; 9:16; 15:26; 21:13) and is used in reference to believers who are undergoing persecution. The fifth instance of this phrase in the New Testament occurs in Romans 15:18, where Paul writes of the grace he received in bringing the Gentiles to faith "for the sake of the Name." This verse reflects more closely how John uses this phrase in 3 John 7.[16] "The Name" in these verses refers to the name of Jesus Christ found in the exclusive message of the gospel. The task of bearing the name of Christ carries with it both honor and humility. Yarbrough illustrates how this plays out in a missiological context when he writes,

> Muslim converts in Islamic countries seeking to bear Christian witness without social compromise can appreciate John's commendation of these gritty gospel servants. Paul's insistence on working for his own upkeep, refusing to receive aid from most churches he planted and served, points to even more rigorous scruples. Jesus sent out his own disciples with the expectation that God would provide their needs through local resources they would encounter.[17]

In place of any form of payment from non-believers, the reward for the ministry of these itinerant preachers was service to Christ (although the New Testament also teaches that ministers of the gospel should be compensated by those to whom they minister—see Luke 10:7; 1 Corinthians 9:9–14).

Finally, John exhorts Gaius in verse 8 that "we ought to support people like these, that we may be fellow workers for the truth." Akin reflects on the responsibility of the church in this matter. He writes, "'ought' (opheilomen) speaks of an obligation. It is our dutiful responsibility. The verb is present tense, and therefore [emphasizes] a continual obligation."[18] The church has the primary, and sometimes sole, responsibility to support gospel workers. As

---

15 Glenn W. Barker, "1, 2, & 3 John,", *The Expositor's Bible Commentary*, vol. 12, ed. Frank E. Gaebelein (Grand Rapids: Zondervan, 1981), 373.

16 Kruse, 223–24.

17 Yarbrough, 373.

18 Akin, 245.

John Stott argues, "We must do for them what others will not do. An important principle lies buried here, namely that we Christians should finance Christian enterprises which the world will not or should not be expected to support."[19] Such support from the church carries both a temporal and an eternal weight. Yarbrough stresses the value of support when he states,

> John would go on to say why such support is a worthy goal: "in order that we might be co-workers for the truth." Synergoi (the word for "support") is used elsewhere in the New Testament about Paul's co-workers Priscilla and Aquila, Titus, Epaphroditus, and Philemon. The list is a helpful reminder of the high privilege of participation in the apostolic mission.[20]

Sometimes your strategy for care will determine who you support and how many you support. When I first came on church staff, the list of missionaries the church supported was a mile long. Unfortunately, this meant that, in many cases, the care we gave was only an inch deep. Over time, our mission team and staff had to begin praying and thinking through how we could provide deeper care for fewer partners. We knew some would look at this approach and say we weren't doing enough, but for long-standing care to happen, it's better to know your missionaries intimately so you can develop and maintain honesty, transparency, and accountability in the relationship. This approach meant that our missionaries were more than just a name on a page. It also allowed us to invest more heavily in our partners, which meant they didn't have to return to the US as often and spend their time visiting churches to raise support. Finally, it increased our church's interest and involvement in our partnerships with sent ones. This kind of participation commends the gospel and its ministers, even as John commends Gaius at the outset of this letter.

Theological Foundations

These four verses provide a theological foundation for why churches should send missionaries out for the sake of the Name. As individuals believe the gospel and are gathered into a local body, the church goes forth on mission to proclaim that same gospel. This passage also encourages not only sending and supporting in isolation but also doing so in community. Steve Jennings, pastor of Immanuel Church in Fujairah, United Arab Emirates, writes, "The Scriptures give us a pattern of discipling and sending out. This

19 Stott, 231.
20 Yarbrough, 374.

should be the normal life of a church so that when the younger Christians witness the older Christians walk this path, they better understand what path they have to walk."[21] While some members go, others stay. Akin writes, "We may not physically go where they go, but when we support them, we go with them anyway. We work together, as one, for the truth. Some give support and some are sent. Both are essential."[22] This principle aligns with the rhythm of recruiting, raising up, and releasing that Jesus talks about when he calls us to "pray earnestly to the Lord of the harvest to send forth laborers into his harvest" (Luke 10:2).

Application to Ministry

Third John provides a biblical basis for why and how the local church should serve as the conduit through which the gospel spreads around the world. Pastor and author Andy Johnson asserts from this passage that "support for missionaries is normal, cooperation among churches is encouraged, knowing whom churches ought to support is critical, and support should be abundant."[23]

A number of implications from this passage can be drawn out to help a local church develop a missionary care strategy for its members in cross-cultural service. First, as local church leaders consider who to support, they must assess well and do so in categories that reveal a person's character, fruitfulness, and biblical knowledge. Elders and members must also equip those they are sending to ensure they are living out their faith in the areas of hospitality, faithful evangelism, and multiplying disciples. I am grateful for agencies like the IMB and other missions organizations who, while having their own assessments, ask the local church to lead the assessment of would-be missionary candidates before they move forward in the application process. The local church is the primary place where faithful ministry can be lived out, and it provides a context wherein members and elders can be in relationship with the sent one and evaluate their character, competency, and convictions as they progress toward future field work.

Leaders in the local church must realize their responsibility to train sent ones in theology, ecclesiology, missiology, and in practical expressions of local and global ministry. When I was serving in a local church, I led a ten-week missions seminar for our aspiring sent ones that walked through the biblical basis for missions, missions history, healthy ecclesiology, and best practices

---

21 Steve Jennings, "What Would Happen if You Sent Your Best?" *9 Marks Journal: Missions* (Fall 2015): 41–42.

22 Akin, 245.

23 Andy Johnson, *Missions: How the Local Church Goes Global* (Wheaton: Crossway, 2017), 38–40.

for missions. We also had a missions reading group in which we read books and other resources on theology, ecclesiology, and missiology. These helped create missions and theological awareness, and they also helped the participants build a healthy foundation to work from on the field. By investing in the training of sent ones, local churches will have a good grasp of their character, faithfulness in ministry, and knowledge of the Bible before they leave, and they will have a better understanding of how to tailor missionary care to each of their long-term workers once they are on the field.

Conclusion

Successful sports recruiting often results in committed athletes being launched to compete at the next level. How much more exciting is it to see churches invite their members into deep, abiding relationships, and then send them out to the nations? The local church must pursue believers whom God might be calling overseas, and they need to be ready to receive, eager to equip, truth-filled in training, and generous in giving and caring for those who go for the sake of Name. When the sending church and her missionaries have a shared commitment and rapport from the outset, missionary care will be evidenced in deep and meaningful ways.

CHAPTER 2

Missionary Care in Philippians 2:25–30

I have thought it necessary to send to you Epaphroditus my broth-er and felloaw worker and fellow soldier, and your messenger and minister to my need, for he has been longing for you all and has been distressed because you heard that he was ill. Indeed he was ill, near to death. But God had mercy on him, and not only on him but on me also, lest I should have sorrow upon sorrow. I am the more eager to send him, therefore, that you may rejoice at seeing him again, and that I may be less anxious. So receive him in the Lord with all joy, and honor such men, for he nearly died for the work of Christ, risking his life to complete what was lacking in your service to me.

As noted from 3 John 5–8 in the previous chapter, the local church func-tions as a greenhouse for raising up and sending out faithful laborers to the harvest field. As church leaders and members identify and evaluate poten-tial missionaries, the church can heartily affirm, commission, and provide ongoing support to those they send out. The relationships between mission-aries and those back home will run deeper if they are formed first at the local church level. Sending should not be the finish line but instead the start of the role the church plays in undergirding the work of her partners. Such mission-ary care continues once workers have arrived on the field.

We see an individual and corporate example of this kind of relation-ship in the New Testament record of Paul's missionary journeys. The book of Acts depicts Barnabas and Paul as faithful members of the church of Antioch before they were sent out by the church. As they and other individuals evan-gelized, discipled, and planted churches, Paul wrote about the partnership he experienced with new believers gathered in local churches. The "gold stan-dard" for a missionary partnership is the church in Philippi. By examining Philippians 2:25–30, we'll discover the biblical and theological context for Paul's partnership with this church (and specifically with one of their own,

Epaphroditus) and how missionary care serves to further the proclamation of the gospel message and establishment of churches.

Background

Founding of the Church

Paul arrived in Philippi in AD 49 and evangelized the first members of the church (Acts 16:11–40). Gordon Fee notes that three of the four founding members of the church were of Greek descent (Lydia, Euodia, and Syntyche), while the fourth, Clement, was of Roman heritage. This diverse group included the wealthy, a slave girl, and those of high position, such as the jailer. Fee explains that, while we cannot know how long Paul and his companions stayed in Philippi, a close bond formed between him and the church that continued in part because of Luke staying in Philippi after Paul departed.[24]

Themes of the Book

The book of Philippians includes many themes such as joy and unity, but Fee describes it as an "hortatory letter of friendship."[25] The partnership was strong from the outset and unlike any other Paul had or would experience. In 4:15, Paul highlights the type of relationship he had with the church when he writes, "And you Philippians yourselves know that in the beginning of the gospel, when I left Macedonia, no church entered into partnership with me in giving and receiving, except you only." A theme of joy amid poverty that leads to generosity echoes throughout the letter, which Paul wrote while imprisoned for preaching the gospel.

Occasion for Sending Epaphroditus

A reader of Paul's letters can confidently conclude that he believed preaching the gospel was worth the cost, and Paul certainly endured considerable hardship during his ministry. The Philippian church saw an opportunity to encourage Paul in his suffering by sending Epaphroditus. The church, aware of Paul's need and their spiritual responsibility to him, sent Epaphroditus with a gift to assist Paul and aid him for a period of time. In turn, by commending Epaphroditus to them, Paul continues the missionary report he gave in 1:12–26 and reveals a desire for the Philippians to take note of

---

24 Gordon D. Fee, *Paul's Letter to the Philippians*, NICNT (Grand Rapids: Eerdmans, 1995), eBook edition, ch. 3, sec. IV.

25 Ibid.

Epaphroditus's example.[26] Gerald Hawthorne and Ralph Martin similarly mention the upholding of Epaphroditus's example: "[Paul] does this not only to inform the Philippians about one of their own, but to provide them with still another striking illustration of the self-sacrificing service that is demanded of all Christians and is so markedly the central theme of the letter (Phil 1:28–30)."[27] We want to explore Epaphroditus's example further, as it gives churches and missionaries a model for the reciprocal nature that partnerships require. Given the focus of this book, we'll limit our study to the parts of this passage that speak directly to missionary care.

Exegetical Context

"My brother and fellow worker and fellow soldier" (v. 25b)

Paul commended Epaphroditus by using titles that speak to his role among the Philippians. According to Stephen Voorwinde, Paul's use of these titles was a direct challenge to the pagan culture of Philippi. He writes that "it is precisely because of his sacrificial service that Epaphroditus is worthy of the titles that Paul lavishes on him." He further points out that, among missionary companions, Paul otherwise only uses the term "brother" for Titus in 2 Corinthians 2:13.[28] This is a familial term and exposes the relationship these men shared.

Of the term "co-worker," Joseph Hellerman says, "Sunergon is a favorite of Paul's to identify co-worker . . . sunergos, unlike adelphos, is not used of believers in general . . . here it may imply that he knew Epaphroditus previously, perhaps as one of the founding members of the Philippian church, who later joined Paul's mission."[29] Epaphroditus likely worked as part of the larger team alongside Paul for the advancement of the gospel.[30] Brotherly affection and a bond based on a shared mission again reveal the closeness of this relationship.

Sending churches can build on their relationship with sent ones by ensuring that healthy communication continues with the mission agen-

26 Moisés Silva, *Philippians*, BECNT, 2nd ed. (Grand Rapids: Baker Academic, 1992, 2005), 4, 134.

27 Gerald F. Hawthorne and Ralph P. Martin, *Philippians*, WBC, Rev. ed. 43, ed. Bruce M. Metzger, David A. Hubbard, and Glenn W. Barker (Grand Rapids: Zondervan, 2004), eBook edition.

28 Stephen Voorwinde, "More of Paul's Emotions in Philippians," *The Reformed Theological Review* 77, no. 1 (April 2018): 45–67.

29 Joseph H. Hellerman, *Exegetical Guide to the Greek New Testament: Philippians*, ed. Andreas J. Köstenberger and Robert W. Yarbrough (Nashville: Broadman & Holman, 2015), 156.

30 Walter G. Hansen, *Philippians*, PNTC (Grand Rapids, Eerdmans, 2009), 202.

cy and the field team. Churches' care ought to include ongoing dialogue with their missionaries—before, during, and after they serve on the field. For example, since conflict between teammates is one of the top two reasons why missionaries come home early, churches can communicate with the agency and the team on the field to make sure they are sending their missionaries into contexts with the chemistry, competencies, and convictions necessary for them to thrive. We see the value this kind of intentionality played in Paul's ministry, and churches should aim to provide the same intentional care today.

Finally, Paul gives Epaphroditus the title "fellow soldier." Hellerman states that this term evokes images of a wounded comrade sent home to rest up and recover.[31] This term describes well the partnership Paul and Epaphroditus had in a spiritual battle.

"And your messenger and minister to my need" (v. 25c)

Paul shifts from terms that reflect the gift of his relationship with Epaphroditus to the role that his friend carried out for the church in Philippi. Edgar Krentz, speaking of the way Epaphroditus served an ambassadorial function, says, "The ambassador acts in the interest of the sending group. Ambassadors came from the elite wealthy in a community; they paid their own expenses when they functioned as ambassadors."[32]

Epaphroditus also worked on behalf of the church as a "minister" to Paul. The care that he showed in meeting Paul's material needs reflects the function the priests carried out for the people during this time.[33] As an ambassador or an advocate, the sending church can extend care and meet real temporal needs. These needs exist within one's physical family, and they exist within one's spiritual family as well. Missionaries should be seen as an extension of the church's membership that are living and ministering in another context. As that relationship is realized, it should be matched with appropriate care. Richard Melick reflects on this point: "The action demonstrated the love of the church in sending and supporting Paul, and it showed the self-giving character of Epaphroditus who left home to serve in difficult circumstances."[34] Such action mirrors what Paul writes elsewhere of Christ's sacrificial nature in going to the cross, which serves as the foundation for

31 Hellerman, 157.

32 Edgar Krentz, "Civic Culture and the Philippians," *Currents in Theology and Mission 35*, no. 4 (August 2008): 258–263.

33 Stephen E. Fowl, *Philippians*, The Two Horizons New Testament Commentary (Grand Rapids: Eerdmans, 2005), 136.

34 Richard R. Mileck Jr., *Philippians*, Colossians, Philemon, NAC 32 (Nashville: Broadman & Holman, 1991), 120.

partnership.

"For he has been longing for you all and has been distressed" (v. 26a)

Despite the service Epaphroditus carried out for Paul and the Philippians, he longed to return to his church. While the timing of his return is unclear, we read later that Epaphroditus became ill and entered great distress. Ralph Martin writes that the phrase "longs for you all" (epipothōn) mirrors the term used for Paul's longing to see the Philippians once more, and "has been distressed" (adēmonōn) is the same word used to describe Jesus's agony in Gethsemane. Although Paul does not specify the cause of Epaphroditus's longing, it's possible he was homesick, or that he was concerned about the church he was separated from, or that he wanted to be back to defend Paul and his message.[35] Regardless of the particular reason(s) he longed for them, the surrounding verses reveal Epaphroditus's desire to be back with the church and report to them all that was carried out on their behalf.

"Indeed he was ill, near death. But God had mercy on him" (v. 27a)

Gospel partnership is not immune to pain, but the hand of God upholds his laborers. David Garland provides a word picture for Epaphroditus being "near death" when he says that "he was 'next door neighbor' (paraplēsious) . . . and it nearly cost him his life."[36] Stephen Fowl reminds the reader that despite the illness, Epaphroditus came to Paul's aid and experienced healing in the process by the mercy of God. He states, "Paul's assertion about God's mercy clearly situates Epaphroditus, his mission, and its ultimate success within God's economy."[37] God's hand guided Paul's circumstances, Epaphroditus's condition, and the church at Philippi for the sake of the gospel being furthered and God's messenger to the Gentiles being strengthened and encouraged.

Missionary care is costly. Just as sent ones count the cost to minister in a cross-cultural setting, so too should senders and supporters count the cost of being spent for the sake of those they send. This may not mean those going to provide missionary care put their life on the line, but it might mean taking a care trip and giving a missionary couple a date night by watching their kids. One of the deepest partnerships in the church I served resulted in part from one of these types of care trips. A mom and son, along with a young adult who had a deep relationship with this missionary family, were able to visit

---

35 Ralph Martin, *Philippians*, TNTC, 3rd ed. 11 (Downers Grove, IL: InterVarsity Press, 1959, 1987, 2008), 138-39.

36 David E. Garland, *Ephesians–Philemon*, EBC, Rev. ed. 12. ed. Tremper Longman III and David E. Garland (Grand Rapids: Zondervan, 1981, 2006), 230.

37 Fowl, 137.

them together. They provided mutual encouragement to one another and were able to build up this family during a time of intense spiritual warfare. It was incredible to hear testimony from this missionary family of the encouragement brought to them in such a critical time. The mom had written notes for seven years to encourage these missionaries and was now able to see these partners on the field and build them up in person. As we see in the relationship between Paul and Epaphroditus, this type of care brings great rewards and results in lasting bonds.

"Not only on him, but on me also, lest I should have sorrow upon sorrow" (v. 27b)

The mercy of God extended not only to Epaphroditus, but also to Paul. He expressed great sorrow at sending Epaphroditus back. Gordon Fee points to the juxtaposition created between the sorrow Paul notes here and the theme of joy that permeates the letter. He writes, "Joy does not mean the absence of sorrow, but the capacity to rejoice in the midst of it. His gratitude in the present case is for mercy, that he has not had sorrow of this kind—the loss of a long-time dear brother in the Lord—added to the sorrow he already knows."[38] Paul could rejoice, even as he exhorted the Philippians to do, because his brother, co-worker, and fellow soldier fulfilled the work the church sent him to accomplish.

I'm sure you've experienced, as I have, the attachment you feel to your sent ones after you've spent time serving alongside them. You become like family in a short time and wish you could stay longer. It's these times, whether it's a week, a month, or even longer, that enable you to build relationships, dive deep into conversations, and build healthy bridges for continued care long after you return.

"I am the more eager to send him . . . that you may rejoice at seeing him again" (v. 28a)

The hope that the Philippians would rejoice at seeing their minister and messenger again underscored Paul's eagerness to send him. Paul can send his friend back in light of a near-death experience and feels less sorrow because the Philippians will receive him with joy.[39] Ultimately, Paul's concern is not the happiness of the believers in Philippi; instead, as Walter Hansen writes, "[Paul's] focus in this passage is always God-centered; rejoicing in Paul's theology is praise for God's mercy and delight in God's presence."[40] Paul

38 Fee, ch. 3, sec. IV.
39 Fowl, 138.
40 Hansen, 207.

turned the focus from the gift he received in Epaphroditus to how the Philippians should now receive him back.

"So receive him in the Lord with all joy, and honor such men" (v. 29)

The crescendo of Paul's commendation reaches its peak in this verse as he says the Philippians should receive Epaphroditus with joy and honor his service. Gordon Fee and Christopher Fowl both note that the church receiving him back with joy does not point to a failed mission; rather, it affirms that "he has fulfilled exemplary Christian duties, even putting his life in danger, and his reception should befit that."[41] Where the Greco-Roman society bestowed honor for civic duty or military prowess, Paul urged the Philippians to show honor to Epaphroditus for giving attention to another's need (an echo of 2:5–11).[42] In more modern language, Hansen states that Paul is "[urging] them to give Epaphroditus a really great banquet and a permanent place of honor rather than a simple potluck supper and a quick nod for his service."[43] Paul received this "sent one" who served with humility and honor, and now he exhorts the church to receive him back with humility and honor.

Churches ought to provide opportunities to hear from teams after they return from the field. This could look like having them share during a morning service or for an extended period of time during the evening service. Another great option is setting up a schedule to have them visit different Bible study groups or in-home small groups, since they provide a more intimate setting for sharing and asking questions. Providing these opportunities is a way of commending those who gave of their time and gifts to labor alongside long-term sent ones, and it also creates a mobilization opportunity to bring others into that partnership through prayer, financial support, and service on future trips. These debrief times for teams can also expose areas of need where the church can lean in and provide more meaningful care. Above all, it's a great way to advocate for the partner on the field and strengthen the relational bonds between the sender and the sent one.

"For he nearly died for the work of Christ, risking his own life to complete . . . your service to me." (v. 30)

What the Philippians could not do because of their physical separation from Paul, Epaphroditus fulfilled on their behalf. David Garland frames this verse in the context of the rest of the letter when he writes, "Paul sets up Epaphroditus as one who follows the example of Christ in his service of

41 Fowl, 138.
42 Ibid.
43 Hansen, 208.

the gospel. As Christ's obedience to God led him 'to death,' Epaphroditus's obedience in carrying out the work of Christ led him to the point of death (2:30)."[44] Epaphroditus was willing to count the cost and sacrifice his life to do what the church could not do in full. Richard Melick Jr. writes that the term "lack" (hysterēma) does not mean they had failed in something but, rather, that the church could do much more by sending Epaphroditus than if they had not.[45] As Gordon Fee concludes, "The passage echoes with notes of gratitude and joy . . . hints at Paul's sorrow . . . and is full of affection and honor for one who dared to risk his life 'for the sake of Christ.'"[46] Not only did Paul receive the gift they sent (4:18), but he also received a gift in the presence of his partner, who served as a model of sacrificial partnership.

Theological Foundations

In Ephesians 4:1, Paul writes to the church at Ephesus that they should "walk in a manner worthy of the calling to which they have been called." He later exhorts the church at Corinth to remember their role as individuals of one body, the local church, and, as such, that they have been called to suffer alongside, rejoice, and honor each other because they have covenanted with one another in membership (1 Cor 12:26). Epaphroditus's story illustrates these same realities. As Paul notes, Epaphroditus completed what lacked in the Philippians' absence. This statement stresses the sense of obligation believers have to one another. As believers in Christ, we are commanded to care for one another. Stephen Fowl states, "Our baptism joins us to a 'family' in which we inevitably will encounter 'lack' which our familial connections oblige us to 'fill up'."[47] Paul's words in this passage stress the importance of the local church's commitment to one another, particularly as it is demonstrated in the way we meet each other's needs.[48] Epaphroditus displayed the mind of Christ in his actions, and Paul reminded the church at Philippi that they should follow his example in how they supported those sent out to further the witness of the gospel.

This passage also provides a biblical foundation for a theology of suffering. Paul and Epaphroditus both embody what it means to count the cost and endure suffering. They faithfully served despite the suffering they faced and continued to depend upon the mercy of God. Sorrow and suffering are normal in the Christian life. As Walter Hansen states, "Rejoicing in the Lord

44 Garland, 231.
45 Mileck Jr., 121.
46 Fee, ch. 3, sec. IV.
47 Fowl, 140.
48 Ibid., 142.

does not mean denying the reality of sorrow caused by tragic circumstances in life."[49] Missionaries often feel isolated and alone, and those feelings are even more acute during a season of suffering. Whether it's an unsettled child, teammate conflict, having to face the reality of aging parents stateside, or homesickness, struggles on the field give the church and her leadership an opportunity to weep with those who weep.

I recall when a missionary called and asked me to check on her elderly father. I quickly responded by making a pastoral visit, and I encouraged others who knew him well to stop by and visit him. He reported this care back to his daughter on the field, which gave her great comfort and assurance that someone was looking out for her family in her absence. This is how churches can provide solace in the midst of suffering. Epaphroditus and Paul found strength in the midst of suffering, which allowed them to give their lives as a pleasing offering to the Lord.

Application to Ministry

Churches tend to see commissioning as the culmination of their job rather than the beginning of the ongoing care they will provide to their missionaries. By considering the example of Epaphroditus, we see a church committed to sending their best, even amidst suffering and hardship, to encourage and hold the rope for a partner they held close. Paul did not exist "out of sight, out of mind" for the church at Philippi, and they took the initiative in caring for him by sending a co-laborer to bless, enrich, and edify Paul in his service.

Looking at the wider context of this passage, we see that Epaphroditus also met a practical need by delivering a financial gift to Paul from the Philippian church (Phil 4:18). Additionally, he served for a period of time as an extension of Paul's long-term work and represented his local church. As local churches consider how to serve their missionaries, prayer, finances, practical skills, counseling sessions, tangible gifts, and "people support" are all means for providing ongoing care. Churches ought to take their cue from the Philippian church when considering short-term mission trips, as sometimes member care trips are the best way to express support and provide encouragement in the work. The church must support their missionaries and not neglect the work of providing ongoing care, as doing so paves the way for profitable, lasting fruit.

49 Hansen, 206.

Conclusion

Relationships are the bedrock of partnership. A strong relationship existed between Paul and the church at Philippi, and that same type of relationship should be seen in present contexts as well. Churches need to develop meaningful relationships with their missionaries as they equip and train them to be biblically faithful workers whom they know and can send with confidence, like the "fellow workers for the truth" we looked at in 3 John 8. Only then can these relationships continue to strengthen as partners leave and begin serving on the field. The church at Philippi could stand behind Epaphroditus, send him with conviction, and, in time, receive him back in an honoring way. They knew how he would care for Paul, and considering the suffering he endured, they knew they should commend him at his return. Through the missionary care they provided for Paul, the Philippians exemplified how to support the furtherance of the gospel by caring for those they sent to the field.

CHAPTER 3

Missionary Care in Acts 14:26–28

[A]nd from there they sailed to Antioch, where they had been commended to the grace of God for the work that they had fulfilled. And when they arrived and gathered the church together, they declared all that God had done with them, and how he had opened a door of faith to the Gentiles. And they remained no little time with the disciples.

As noted in the survey of 3 John 5–8 and Philippians 2:25–30 in chapters 1 and 2, missionary care begins prior to sending missionaries to the field and continues throughout their ministry. This support carried out by the local church expands into a third facet of care as missionaries return home for stateside assignment—whether planned, unplanned, or in their concluding years of service through retirement. By exploring the biblical context, theological foundation, and ministry application of Acts 14:26–28, we will see how the local church can provide this third avenue of missionary care after their missionaries have returned from the field.

Background

Throughout the book of Acts, the task of seeing the gospel move from Jerusalem to the ends of the earth (Acts 1:8) is carried out, first by the apostles, but ultimately in the establishment of local congregations. Whereas the people of God were forcibly scattered in their witness due to persecution in Acts 8, there is a very intentional sending that takes place in Acts 13. As Darrell Bock notes, "The call of Barnabas and Paul takes place in the context of worship . . . everything about the event argues that mission is grounded in God's command and the response of a church engaged in devotion. The Spirit directs that the two be sent out, and the church is obedient to the call."[50] Paul and Barnabas set out in obedience to the Holy Spirit and the commission of their church. Eckhard Schnabel summarizes their ministry:

> The missionary work of Paul and Barnabas takes place in a context of opposition and persecution; it is accompanied by signs and wonders; it challenges religious ideas that confuse God and the world; it proclaims the living God and his grace; and it nurtures new churches through structural consolidation and sending through missionary information.[51]

God uses Paul and Barnabas as his vessels to see new converts and churches established.

Paul and Barnabas remained committed to their call despite setbacks, knowing God would use them to bring about his redemptive purposes. Regarding Acts 14, David Peterson writes, "Although there have been several accounts of persecution so far in Luke's narrative, the pastoral application in these verses functions to challenge readers . . . [F]aith is also an important theme in the chapter, illustrating the claim that God had 'opened a door of faith to the Gentiles.'"[52] As they conclude their first journey, this is the testimony that Paul and Barnabas take back to Antioch where they were first commissioned.

Exegetical Context

After concluding their first missionary journey through Cyprus, South Galatia, and Pamphylia, Paul and Barnabas returned to the church at Antioch, where they "spent no little time" with the members and reported how God had used them (14:26–28). Both in sending out "sent ones" and receiving them back, the church at Antioch reflects the local church's crucial role in caring for missionaries through sending, supporting, and receiving. Darrell Bock simply and powerfully states that "Mission drives the dynamic community that Luke describes."[53] Paul and Barnabas, set apart and sent out by the church at Antioch in Acts 13:1–3, carry out their first missionary journey by planting churches and establishing elders. Schnabel notes three truths in this section (13:1–14:28): "The two missionaries have faithfully carried

---

50 Darrell L. Bock, *Acts*, BECNT (Grand Rapids: Baker, 2007), 438.

51 Eckhard J. Schnabel, *Acts*, ZECNT (Grand Rapids: Zondervan, 2012), 596–97.

52 David G. Peterson, *The Acts of the Apostles*, PNTC (Grand Rapids: Eerdmans, 2009), 402.

53 Darrell L. Bock, *A Theology of Luke and Acts: Biblical Theology of the New Testament* (Grand Rapids: Zondervan, 2012), 308.

out their mission, so they return to the church that sent them . . . the proclamation of the gospel is the 'work' . . . [and] the conversions of the Jews and Gentiles and establishment of new congregations was the result of the grace of God."[54] Upon their return, they report back to the very church that had commended them to the grace of God, share all that God had done through them, and express how a door of faith had been opened to the Gentiles (Acts 14:26–27).

David Peterson highlights how 14:26 represents the culmination of the commissioning that happened back in chapter 13. He writes,

> First, [Luke] records that they had been 'handed over to the grace of God' *(paradedemenoi tē chartiti tou theou)* for the work which was now completed. Here the grace of God refers to God's protective care and his enabling ministry. Secondly, *they gathered the church together and reported all that God had done through them,* suggesting that the whole church had been involved in sending them out, in response to God's call.[55]

Bock underscores the commitment of this church to their missionaries: "Antioch is described as a church that 'commended' *(paradedomenoi)* them to God's grace. The expression could also translate as 'committed to stress God's care.' The point is that they were handed over to God."[56] The commitment of the sender and the sent is evident in both the church's reliance on God in their support of Paul and Barnabas, and also in Paul and Barnabas's decision to return and report to their sending church.[57]

Peterson notes that this reporting was an encouragement to the believers and to Paul and Barnabas themselves. He writes, "Reporting back was a way of encouraging those believers to see how God in his grace had been answering their prayers. Reviewing their experiences, Paul and Barnabas were able to see the hand of God in everything that had happened."[58] Paul and Barnabas's report reflects what God did through them, which led most notably to the door of faith opened to the Gentiles. Bock explains this imagery: "It is the Gentile mission that is the focus of the report, as through a door into a new place. The point of the metaphor here is access to God. The image of the

54 Schnabel, *Acts*, 615.

55 Peterson, 416.

56 Bock, *Acts*, 484.

57 Ibid. Bock emphasizes that "church" in this verse is a singular noun (tēn ekklēsian), pointing to its corporate unity and how the entire community shared in the sending. The implication therein is that the role of sending is not just relegated to the paid staff of the church but extends to the entire congregation.

58 Peterson, 416.

door *(thyra)* for evangelism is common for Paul."[59]

The return of Paul and Barnabas to the church at Antioch gives us a picture of accountability in mission partnerships and demonstrates the reciprocal nature of care. These men recognized their responsibility to speak back into the life of the church, both by commending the church for their support and by communicating all that God had done through them. In turn, the church at Antioch gained a greater understanding of Paul and Barnabas's missionary efforts and of how to provide care for those they sent out.

I get most energized by being on the field with missionaries, but a close second is hearing from them while they are stateside. Walking alongside them as they readjust to their "home" culture, providing a listening ear, and commending them for their service helps build their confidence and gives honor and care where it is due. The church should not only seek to hear about the work but also about how the missionaries are doing, thereby fulfilling their responsibility to continue discipling their sent ones, both on and off the field.

Finally, the quality of their report matched the quantity of time spent nurturing the Antioch believers. As Peterson concludes, "The importance placed on the pastoral care of churches is once again indicated by mention of their long stay with the disciples at Antioch (*chronon ouk oligon*, 'no little time')."[60] Paul and Barnabas spoke into the life of the church during their stay to encourage, exhort, and mobilize this body by reporting what God had accomplished and would accomplish through their sending and supporting.

Theological Foundations

This passage reveals the fruit of all that the church at Antioch labored toward. After identifying, assessing, and equipping Paul and Barnabas for the missionary task, they sent them off, supported them through prayers and financial gifts, and received them back into the fold. Bock emphasizes the need for the church to send out their best, knowing that the Lord will raise others to carry on the work. He states, "Communities formed are not ignored once their founders move on. Rather, there is an abiding connection that also means that return visits can take place. Too many communities lose track of those they send . . . or missionaries leave a community and are never heard from again."[61] The church in Antioch did not have an "out-of-sight, out-of-mind" attitude, but one of vested relationship and committed partnership.

59 Bock, *Acts*, 484.
60 Peterson, 416.
61 Bock, *Acts*, 484.

Naturally, the church rejoiced at the report of the ways God used Paul and Barnabas as instruments for his purposes. Craig Keener states, "Reporting God's mighty works back to the Antioch church (14:27) fits Luke's pattern of retelling divine deeds within the story . . . and attributing these works to God."[62] The testimony of missionaries helps people see the faithfulness of God in bringing about his redemptive purposes and using human means to accomplish those ends.

Application to Ministry

The sending church should be seen as a haven for reporting, resting, and recharging as missionaries come off the field. Much like a coach pulls an exhausted player off the field to protect them and foster their longevity over the course of the game, the church needs to be a place where missionaries are received into the tangible care of those who know them, support them, and love them deeply. This post-field, reentry care is expressed in tangible ways such as providing lodging, transportation, and opportunities for counseling and equipping. Look for ways you can bless your missionaries in tangible ways, such as by providing missionary housing while they are stateside. Not every church has a dedicated house at their disposal for this purpose, but if you can find a place to house your missionaries—whether in a member's spare room, an apartment unit, or an AirBnB—you will provide a great blessing and relieve a great burden from them. Having a space to retreat, rest, and refocus will help refuel your missionaries for the work ahead.

As in the story of Paul and Barnabas, churches should also provide time for their missionaries to speak to the church, both to express appreciation and to encourage them to further their commitment to pray, send, give, and go. Why is it that we are attracted to the journals of a David Brainerd or a Jim Elliot? Because we love reading the stories—both the ups and downs—and getting a glimpse into the reality of life on the field. The church should be the place for real and, often, raw reporting that gives the rest of the church a chance to join in the adventures and agonies of their brothers and sisters who labor for the sake of the gospel.

Conclusion

The examples seen in John's third epistle, the church at Philippi, and the church at Antioch stress the mutual benefit born out of missionary care that

---

62 Craig S. Keener, *Acts: An Exegetical Commentary*, vol. 2: Acts 3:1–14:28 (Grand Rapids: Baker Academic, 2013), 2191.

begins before missionaries are sent, extends throughout their service, and continues when they return home. As Bock writes, "Missionaries are not to be sent, gone, and forgotten; a line of communication is to remain so that both communities can be connected and blessed by seeing how God is working and binding them together."[63] The sending sometimes hurts, the service can be taxing, and the return is often bittersweet, but in every moment, care should be consistent. Thankfully, God has given us these examples in his Word of how churches can and should care for those they send out for the sake of the Name.

63 Bock, *Acts*, 484.

Ministry Foundations of Missionary Care

This section will focus on the ministry foundations necessary for developing a strategy to assist the local church in caring for its missionaries. Chapter 4 gives an overview of the church's responsibility to its missionaries. We'll define missionary care and explain its importance, then we'll review both theoretical and philosophical understandings of missionary care and look at a historical example of the church caring well for its sent ones. Chapter 5 explores the role of the local church in missionary care by evaluating responses from missionaries, local churches, and missionary care personnel. Chapter 6 provides an evaluation of the role of the agency in missionary care—again from the vantage points of the missionary, local churches, and missionary care personnel.

Chapter 7 contains findings from research on the partnership between the local church and the mission agency. Those findings will help us identify potential gaps in missionary care and best practices for facilitating better care, which should result in better missionary retention. Chapter 8 is a survey of church models that provide some level of care for their missionaries, and chapter 9 concludes this section by reviewing research on healthy markers of missionary care in the pre-field, on-field, and post-field stages. The final chapter is a charge to churches to take hold of the rope and provide meaningful, intentional care for those they send.

To begin to understand the need for missionary care, a foundation for the church's responsibility needs consideration.

CHAPTER 4

The Church's Responsibility to Its Sent Ones

Theoretical Approach

Isolated, overlooked, and undervalued— feelings experienced by nearly every missionary as they settle on the field. The missionary senses a lack of connectivity in their relationship with the church that commissioned them and the culture in which they are seeking to immerse themselves. Pastor David Wilson writes, "When [missionaries] first leave for the field, it is often with a wonderful commissioning and send-off with the prayers of people who know them, love them and appreciate what they're doing. But as the years go by and the busyness of life overtakes those in the home church, good intentions of trust can fall by the wayside."[64] Although churches can't make their missionaries feel more connected to their new culture, by going deeper with fewer missionaries and building in avenues for advocacy, they can strengthen that relational bond between sent ones and their sending church body.

Whereas missionary heroes from centuries past left with all their belongings, knowing they would never see home again, today there are many ways for missionaries to stay connected and even escape (figuratively or literally) back to the familiar. David Joannes, president of Within Reach Global, reflects that for missionaries who are "Unprepared for the immense culture shock they face, abandoning their station often feels like the only option."[65] The goal of those caring for the missionary must be for them to thrive, not just survive. Missiologist Deborah Ford explains, "such understanding of missionary care focuses not only on curative, but also preventative measures . . . the ultimate aim is to develop inner resources within missionaries, as well

---

64 David J. Wilson, ed., *Mind the Gaps: Engaging the Church in Missionary Care* (Colorado Springs: Believers, 2015), 82.

65 David Joannes, *The Mind of a Missionary: What Global Kingdom Workers Tell Us About Thriving on Mission Today* (Prescott, AZ: Within Reach Global, 2015), 130.

as providing external resources to help them with their work."[66] Churches can develop a strategy that focuses on self-awareness for the missionary and also provides practical help for the local church—not just in commissioning, but also in building commitment in both the sent and the sender.

To understand their responsibility for missionary care, the local church first needs to properly define it. Kelly O'Donnell defines missionary care simply as "the investment of resources by mission agencies, sending churches, and related mission organizations to nurture and develop missionary personnel."[67] This definition highlights the multi-layered nature of missionary care as it identifies the three players involved: the missionary, mission agency, and local church. And this multi-layered partnership helps ensure that no facet of missionary care is neglected. As author and missions practitioner Neal Pirolo argues, "Each level has its strengths and weaknesses. Yet, the weakness of one is the strength of another."[68] Deep partnership between all three groups must exist for the missionary to excel in living and laboring for the gospel.

Because of the multiple layers found within missionary care, some have asked who bears the primary responsibility for providing.[69] Pirolo argues that the local church should fill this role: "I believe that we need to begin at the church level because the Great Commission was given to the church."[70] The case for putting the local church at the forefront builds not only from the practical nature of care, but also from the biblical warrant on which this care is grounded. The need for the church to take the lead in providing care was evident in the situation I noted in the introduction, where missionaries sent out by a local church had reached the point of burnout and had come off the field needing counseling. The church could have worked in greater concert with the agency and taken the initiative in pastoring this couple. This is just one example of how the church can be proactively practical in care.

The book of Acts presents the church as the authoritative sending body

66 Deborah M. Ford, "P(r)ay as they Go? Re-examining the Role of the Local Church in Cross-cultural Missionary Care," *Evangel* 22.1 (2004): 4–10.

67 Kelly O'Donnell, *Missionary Care: Counting the Cost for World Evangelization* (Pasadena, CA: William Carey Library, 1992), 10, 286.

68 Neal Pirolo, "Four Levels of Missionary Care: Part One," Upstream Collective, 15 May 2019, https://www.upstreamcollective.org/post/four-levels-of-missionary-care-part-one.

69 Joe Miller, Ben Marshall, and Sandra Murray, "Church Driven Soul Care for Overseas Missionaries," Biblical Counseling Coalition, 24 March 2021, www.biblicalcounselingcoalition.org/2021/03/24/the-local-church-as-an-equipping-and-long-term-care-instrument-for-sending-overseas-missionaries/. Miller, Marshall, and Murray argue that the church, as the pillar and buttress for truth, should stand as the primary player in the soul care of missionaries. They write, "One of the many axioms pertaining to global missions is that God's people will experience both suffering and sin. While missionaries should never be treated as if they are immune to suffering and sin, neither should church leadership minimize or ignore the pressures missionaries face on the field."

70 Pirolo, "Four Levels of Missionary Care: Part One."

of the missionary.[71] However, many in the church do not place a high value on their role as sender. As Zach Bradley says, "We must resist the urge to say that it is better kingdom work there than here . . . Everywhere we are, we serve the Lord."[72] It is a high calling to be a sender and it demands just as much sacrifice, as pictured through the church at Antioch or in the example of Epaphroditus. Churches ought to heed the example found in the church at Philippi and put meaningful effort into caring for their sent ones. O'Donnell notes the burden-bearing work that missionary care requires. He exhorts his readers that "Member care helps to balance the realistic demands of suffering and sacrifice with the realistic needs for support and nurture in our lives . . . we must find additional ways to lighten the load on ourselves and our colleagues. Biblically, the call to take up our cross daily is to also understand that we bear our crosses together."[73] This encouragement toward cross-bearing underscores the reality that we battle spiritually together (cf. Eph 6:10–20), crossing into opposing fields and needing to remain on guard.

I recall a number of such cross-bearing opportunities during my ministry: the single missionary on the field reaching back and expressing feelings of loneliness; the missionary experiencing relational conflict and seeking counsel; or the missionary going into a previously uncontacted area asking for focused prayer. All of these were opportunities to step into the real-life, spiritual world and get in the foxhole together to battle in intercessory prayer.

Missionaries on the field need the investment of their sending church in all circumstances. As David Wilson reminds us, "Our global workers are in harm's way, and they have an enemy who will exploit every spiritual weakness they may have . . . the main priority for the local church is to lead them to develop spiritual muscles that will enable them to thrive on the mission field."[74] Bill Cook and Chuck Lawless describe the ways the missionary experiences Satan's attack on the mission field. They focus on the areas of discouragement, distraction, and destruction, from small annoyances, like lack of preferences, to bigger obstacles, like persecution.[75] Whether it's regarding issues of language acquisition or team compatibility, churches must stand

71 Beirn and Murray, 110. See also Thomas Hale and Gene Daniels, *On Being a Missionary*, rev. ed. (Littleton, CO: William Carey Library, 2012).

72 Zach Bradley, Susan McCrary, Rodney Calfee, and Andy Jansen, *Receiving Sent Ones During Reentry: The Challenges of Coming "Home" and How Churches Can Help* (Upstream Collective: CreateSpace, 2017), Kindle edition, ch. 6, "Words from One Returning Sent One to Another."

73 Kelly O'Donnell, *Global Member Care: The Pearls and Perils of Good Practice*, Vol. 1 (Pasadena, CA: William Carey Library, 2011), 7.

74 Wilson, 117.

75 William F. Cook III and Chuck Lawless, *Spiritual Warfare in the Storyline of Scripture* (Nashville: B&H Academic, 2019), 267–68. Miller, Marshall, and Murray in their article "Church-Driven Soul Care" address similar challenges on the field for missionaries and affirm the need for the church to step in to provide care.

alongside their missionaries to develop trust in God and confidence in their role as the lead sender and support network. As O'Donnell reflects, "Member care, I have learned over and over again, is not about creating a comfortable lifestyle. Nor is it about trusting people instead of trusting God. Rather, it is about further developing the resiliency to do our work well, which includes our character, competencies and social support."[76] There must be a relational resiliency, both among teammates, and between the sender and sent one.

I was greatly encouraged by partners who were willing to open themselves up to exhortation, encouragement, and even rebuke on a personal level, and who sought input on how they could improve in communication or accountability. If the church truly views their missionaries as an extension of the church, then the physical separation between the sent one and the sender shouldn't diminish the spiritual oversight the church can provide. And that ongoing close connection should help the church remain receptive to the missionaries' requests for greater accountability, relational buy-in, and even financial commitment. O'Donnell argues that the relationship is "a 'two-way street,' as both senders and goers have responsibilities to each other."[77] Both the church and the missionary must invest in this partnership. As Beirn writes, "Our personal ownership of the Great Commission mandate does not end where another person's begins. We are to own it together. There is no expiration date on a church or individual fully embracing the Great Commission."[78] This partnership between church and missionary, built upon the biblical model, strengthens as the church receives adequate resources to carry out its role in missionary care.

Philosophical Approach

As churches begin to understand the why and the what of missionary care, they next must understand the how. Beirn and Murray ask, "How do we prepare ourselves to be a sending church in a way that is both workable for us and meaningful for the person inquiring about missions?"[79] In addition to the affirmation of a clear call to the field, missionaries rely on their churches to provide faithful role models to emulate as well as practical resources and relationships. Mission strategist Rob Hay states, "Member care is not an option but an obligation. It is an integrated way of caring for our missionaries that infuses all principles and practices."[80] Such ministry needs to be

76 O'Donnell, *Global Member Care*, 7.

77 Ibid., 10.

78 Beirn and Murray, 42.

79 Ibid., 75.

80 Rob Hay, *Worth Keeping: Global Perspectives on Best Practice in Missionary Retention* (Pasadena, CA: William Carey Library, 2007), 188.

threaded throughout the culture of a church in a way that involves the entire church.

Before the church can determine what facets of missionary care they can provide, they must truly know those they support. The value of care is not in the size of the check written but in the depth of the relationship forged. Member care specialist Jamie Haguewood warns that "You can't care for people you don't actually know, regardless of how much money you send them per month."[81] Meaningful partnership requires a foundational trust that can only be earned and developed through long-term relationships.[82]

There are a number of ways we sought to effectively live this out as a church. One was to highlight our sent ones in a weekly newsletter in which we provided ministry updates and prayer requests. We also included our sent ones in the church's member directory and listed their email addresses (as appropriate) so members could reach out and send a word of encouragement. We regularly prayed for missionaries in the morning service, and we highlighted a missionary unit in every Sunday evening service.

We also took steps to maintain this relational connection through leadership transitions so the partnership would not be negatively impacted. When a new senior pastor joined our church staff, I made sure he had a video conference with each missionary to make that connection and give both parties an opportunity to hear from the other. Taking proactive steps to prevent disrupting the partnership helped maintain the relational bridge between the church and the missionary. As care strategies are developed and adjusted over the years, churches must discipline themselves in the personal, communal, and biblical practice of garnering trust and deepening their relationships with workers on the field.

Missionary care involves not only the initial investment in relationship but also an ongoing care as the partnership continues. As O'Donnell writes, "Member care seeks to implement an adequate flow of care [at every stage of service] from recruitment through retirement."[83] Pirolo highlights five types of care from Paul's ministry: moral support, reentry support, logistics support, communication support, and financial support. He advocates for having individuals in the church who are equipped with field knowledge provide care in each of these areas.[84] Understanding the need to provide care in these areas and the types of stress missionaries experience (cultur-

81 Jamie Haguewood, "Missionaries Abroad Need Friendships Back Home," *Reaching and Teaching Blog*, 8 December 2020, https://rtim.org/missionaries-abroad-need-friendships-back-home/.

82 O'Donnell, *Global Member Care*, 103.

83 Ibid., 10, 47.

84 Pirolo, "Four Levels of Missionary Care: Part One."

al, human, organizational, physical, psychological, support, and spiritual) will help churches persevere in providing meaningful care throughout the pre-field, on-field, and post-field stages of a missionary's career.[85]

While my connection to partners on the field looks different now in a missions mobilization role, I have found that setting up a schedule for communication with missionaries is helpful. Whether once a month, every other month, or at some other interval, scheduling time for regular communication provides accountability and helps both sides prioritize the relationship. I also make a regular practice of responding to missionary newsletters. The reply doesn't have to be long, but a quick note to acknowledge their reporting and affirm your desire to hold the ropes through prayer and support speaks volumes to the missionary. There are myriad ways to demonstrate care and support for those we send out, and not all of them will be practical for your church or applicable to your partnerships. But those who send should take the initiative in seeking out ways to provide meaningful, tangible care to those they have sent.

Note, though, that a church can swing too far on the pendulum of care in such a way that it negatively affects missionary retention. O'Donnell writes, "There is actually a U-shaped correlation between member care and retention: too little and too much member care are both related to lower retention. Perhaps too much member care can actually hinder the development of resilience for mission workers."[86] Nevertheless, churches should aim to provide as much care as they can and then adjust if they find it is too much or too little. And we must remember that retention and longevity are not ends in themselves but means by which God's people persevere in the proclamation of the gospel. O'Donnell exhorts, "Hard places require dedicated, experienced, and committed missionaries . . . it requires well trained workers and quality sending groups with an effective member care system."[87] The pressures of the mission field, the examples we have from missions history, and the pattern of Scripture all provide warrant for giving ongoing care that fosters resilience and retention in missionaries on the field.

Historical Approach

William Carey, known as the "father of the modern missionary movement," exemplified the "no turning back" mentality of a resilient missionary. While delivering a sermon on May 31, 1792, in Nottingham, England,

---

85 O'Donnell, *Global Member Care*, 117–18.
86 Ibid., 43.
87 Ibid., 44–45.

Carey famously exhorted the congregants to *expect great things from God and attempt great things for God.*[88] This encouragement, combined with his famous pamphlet *Enquiry into the Obligations of Christians*, eventually led to the formation of an alliance to support the sending of missionaries. Historian Michael Haykin notes that, despite the clarion call from Carey, the assembly ultimately dismissed his request to be sent out and supported.[89] Carey's missionary companion Josh Marshman, however, mobilized the likes of Andrew Fuller, John Sutcliff, and John Ryland to form the Baptist Missionary Society (an interdenominational society made up of members from various churches) which supported the work of Carey and others to carry the gospel to the ends of the earth.[90] S. Pearce Carey recounts that this group "pledged every care [for he and his family]"[91] and set him apart for the work he had been called to, much as Antioch set apart Barnabas and Saul.[92] They committed then to "hold the rope" on behalf of Carey. Andrew Fuller describes that experience:

> Our undertaking to India really appeared at its beginning to me somewhat like a few men, who were deliberating about the importance of penetrating a deep mine, which had never before been explored. We had no one to guide us; and, whilst we were thus deliberating, Carey, as it were, said, "Well I will go down, if you will hold the rope." But before he descended, he, as it seemed to me, took an oath from each of us at the mouth of the pit, to this effect that "whilst we lived, we should never let go [of] the rope."[93]

The missionary, the society, and the church—all were working together to assist in this effort.

What was it, though, that set this missionary care example apart as one to follow? It was the unending advocacy for and undergirding through prayer of those they supported. The memoirs of Samuel Pearce reflect their labors

88 Zane Pratt, M. David Sills, and Jeff K. Walters, *Introduction to Global Missions* (Nashville: B&H Academic, 2014), 117. Baptist Missionary Society, Periodical Accounts Relative to a Society Formed Among the Particular Baptist for Propagating the Gospel Among the Heathen (London, UK: J.W. Morris, 1800, no. 1 p. 3), http://www.wmcarey.edu/carey/per-acct-vol1/bms-founding.pdf.

89 Michael A.G. Haykin, *The Missionary Fellowship of William Carey* (Sanford, FL: Reformation Trust, 2018), 79.

90 Ibid., 80. See also John Clark Marshman, The Life and Times of Carey, Marshman, and Ward, William Carey University, https:www.wmcarey.edu/carey/jcmarsh-man/lifetimes.htm, 1:15, and Timothy George, *Faithful Witness: The Life and Mission of William Carey* (Birmingham, AL: New Hope, 1991), 33, 135.

91 S. Pearce Carey, *William Carey* (London, UK: Hodder & Stoughton, 1923), 117.

92 S. Pearce Carey, *Samuel Pearce, M.A.*, The Baptist Brainerd (London, UK: The Carey Press, 1934), 142.

93 Carey, *William Carey*, 118.

in prayer, as he wrote to Carey, "We love you in the bowels of Christ, and we ardently pray for you every day . . . daily in our closets and in our families do we remember you before God; and in the sanctuary, [we] wrestle hard for you Sabbath after Sabbath."[94] His sending and supporting churches also demonstrated advocacy by reading his letters aloud from the pulpit.[95] Carey, much like Paul and Barnabas, took accountability to his sending church seriously, and the church, in turn, advocated selflessly for their sent one.

As Pearce continued hearing about Carey's work in India, he developed a growing desire to be sent if the Lord willed. He writes, "I look at my brother Carey's portrait . . . I love him and long to join his labors." But even if God didn't call him overseas, he knew he still had a part to play in supporting and advancing the mission. "I have resolved . . . that, the Lord helping me, if I cannot go abroad, I will do all I can to serve the mission at home."[96] As David Joannes notes, rope-holding is needed now as much as it was then. He writes,

> William Carey went down into the goldmine of souls in
> India, expecting Christians on the home front to hold the
> ropes. This is still the desire of Kingdom workers today.
> They desire a covering of prayer from sending churches, a
> sincere interest in their unique fields, and a tug on the end
> of the rope when they are surrounded by the darkness of a
> distant missionary life.[97]

Churches must understand their responsibility to care for their sent ones and give of themselves tirelessly and sacrificially to those they send and support.

94 Andrew Fuller, *A Heart for Missions: A Classic Memoir of Samuel Pearce* (Birmingham, AL: Solid Ground Christian Books, 2006), 33, 53.

95 Ibid., 35.

96 Ibid., 96.

97 Joannes, 152.

CHAPTER 5

The Role of the Church in Missionary Care

The church must be seen as the central means by which the Great Commission is carried out. Considering this, how can the local church excel in providing ongoing care to the missionaries it sends and supports? Eric Wright notes that the constant refrain from colleagues on the field was a need for counsel, encouragement, and support from leadership within the church.[98] O'Donnell notes that the church leadership and congregation should provide not only logistical support but also spiritual care for the church's missionaries. He writes, "When our people feel cared for and are growing, they will be more fruitful in their service for the Lord."[99] Those who are poured into and cared for by their sending church will be better equipped to persist and persevere in their labors on the field.

To assess how the church is caring and should care for its sent ones, I conducted surveys among missionaries, local churches, and member care personnel of mission mission agencies. Overall, the responses reflect areas in which missionaries, churches, and agencies are encouraged by the local church's provision and care; however, missionaries feel a lack of engagement from their local church in some particular areas and would be aided by more focused equipping and care.

From the Missionary's Perspective

I surveyed seven missionaries who were sent from various churches and are serving alongside different mission agencies to gain a well-rounded scope of the local church's care from the vantage point of those on the

---

98 Eric E. Wright, *A Practical Theology of Missions: Dispelling the Mystery; Recovering the Passion* (Leominster, UK: Day One, 2018), 232.
99 O'Donnell, *Global Member Care*, 60.

field. The missionaries[100] interviewed (who are all serving alongside various mission agencies) include: Susannah Brock, serving in Europe; Trent and Braidi Brown, serving in South America; Howard and Sharon Harper, serving in Central Asia; Rick and Susan Plummer, serving in Canada; Clark and Christy Smith, serving in South America; and Derek and Jennifer Yancey, serving in South Africa. The survey aimed to have each missionary unit evaluate how the church is excelling in providing missionary care at the pre-field, on-field, and post-field stages, and where there are areas of care in which the church can improve.

Pre-Field Care

The consensus from the field was that, by and large, there is much room for churches to improve in providing meaningful pre-field care. The Yanceys have been serving on the mission field since 2003 and were sent by a Baptist church in Eugene, Oregon. They recount no involvement from their sending church in areas of assessment, equipping, or training. Likewise, the Plummers, sent out by a Baptist church in Harrison, Arkansas, were encouraged by the church during the application process and commissioning but received no assessment to gauge their readiness or equipping for life as a missionary.

Susannah Brock, on the other hand, gave high commendation to her sending church on the pre-field care they provided. She states, "My sending church (in Fayetteville, Arkansas) played a big role in my journey to go overseas. It was there that I learned about the missional heart of God and the importance of every believer either going or sending." She stated that the church's leadership did a thorough job in assessing her call, competencies, and character and gave her opportunities through various trainings and trips to affirm that call.

I had the opportunity to pour into Susannah as she took part in mission equipping courses, mission reading groups, and short-term mission trips to help her gauge her readiness for the mission field. She is an example of one who had an inward desire to be on the field, saw an opportunity to go, and asked her local church to affirm that desire in light of her gifts and current faithfulness in ministry service. As I walked alongside her through equipping opportunities and mission experiences, it was evident that the Lord was preparing her for missionary service.

When asked about where there could be greater accountability and involvement in pre-field care, the Harpers, Plummers, and Yanceys highlighted the areas of equipping and providing mission-field exposure prior to long-

100 I used pseudonyms for these missionaries and generalized their mission agencies, church affiliations, and regions of service for security purposes.

term service. These three missionary units expressed a desire to see churches increase their involvement in equipping missionaries in the areas of evangelism, discipleship training, educating kids in the home, cultural acquisition, and suffering. In addition, they suggested that churches encourage candidates to read missionary biographies and other missions-related texts and participate in trainings like Perspectives to aid in their development. They also felt churches should send those considering missions on short-term trips, as they provide missionary candidates opportunities to experience life on the field and evaluate their commitment to and competency for overseas ministry.

Trent and Braidi Brown encouraged local churches to confirm the Holy Spirit's call on a believer's life and help that missionary candidate in his or her placement, just as the church at Antioch did with Paul and Barnabas. They stressed that the local church is best equipped to see the gifts of sent ones and can, therefore, provide them with the mentorship they need. Brock expressed an interest in mentorship, not only by the local church, but also by seasoned missionaries. Missionaries who took on a "Paul-like" role of equipping and sharing lessons from their life and ministry could have a tremendous impact on potential sent ones. The church where I served on staff had a number of retired missionary units among its membership. I would encourage churches with current or retired missionaries to utilize them to assess future missionary candidates, be an open book for sharing experiences and advice, and be an ongoing stalwart of support for sent ones.

On-Field Care

Among those interviewed, on-field care ranks highest in the three aspects of missionary care the church provides. As we have already established, the local church knows their missionaries best and, therefore, should be able to provide the most well-rounded assessment and care to their missionaries. Rob Hay notes,

> Each local sending church can, and should, offer this kind of a 'family' that is rarely provided by mission agencies. Each missionary can be blessed, not only materially, but with the sense of being loved and cared for. The local church will be blessed by extending its emotional commitments around the world to match in spiritual ones.[101]

Churches should value and foster care in the areas of physical, emotional (whether traumatic or relational), and spiritual well-being. Several mission-

---

101 Hay, 375.

aries noted that prayer is a good starting point for providing on-field care. Churches can care for their missionaries on the field by engaging in both personal prayer and, as illustrated in the example of William Carey, corporate prayer.

The key to on-field missionary care is a strong relationship. The surveyed missionaries noted that regular touchpoints are vital, whether through calls, emails, texts, or in-person visits. Both the Yanceys and Brock highlighted regular touchpoints with the missions pastor of their sending church while on the field, as well as times of debriefing after returning stateside, as meaningful displays of church care. Brock also noted that, while she has had other church members connect with her while she has been home, she would value the broader congregation (beyond just the church leadership) advocating for her while she was on the field. Howard Harper reflected on this as well: "Relational contact [is valued] while on the field, not for a report, a photo, a form to fill out, or a yearly review, but just to say, 'Hi,' feel the pulse of the missionary, and be a listening ear." He noted that going deeper with fewer missionaries allows for stronger relational bonds to be forged.

One valuable and practical avenue that churches can take to have deeper relational touchpoints is to implement advocacy teams. Author Zach Bradley defines advocacy teams/groups in the following way:

> Advocacy groups are four to eight people with a designated leader who commit to providing ongoing support for a particular missionary. They meet regularly to pray for and communicate with the missionary as well as plan things like sending care packages, providing logistical support, setting up visits, and anything else the missionary needs.[102]

Brock highlighted the help and encouragement it would provide to have members of an advocacy team checking in regularly with her and making occasional visits. The Smiths suggested that these advocates could provide correspondence between the missionary and the church and help coordinate logistical support when missionaries return stateside. Brock remarked that she has felt acutely the lack of an advocate team while her sending church transitions to a new missions pastor. No one has picked up the baton of advocacy during this transition, and she has experienced a gap in care as a result. The Yanceys, on the other hand, responded that their sending church has aided in keeping them connected back home in very practical ways, such

---

102 Zach Bradley, "A Practical Way to Structure Your Church's Missionary Care," International Mission Board, 31 May 2017, https://www.imb.org/2017/05/31/practical-way-structure-church-missionary-care/; and Bradley Bell, *The Sending Church Defined*, 2nd ed. (Knoxville, TN: The Upstream Collective, 2015), 145–50.

as by sending them the weekly church-wide emails and providing access to online streaming so they can watch worship services. For both the senders and those who are being sent, it is valuable to have an advocacy relationship in place.

In addition to maintaining regular communication, churches should also make in-person visits to give their missionaries an opportunity to decompress and dialogue with familiar faces from their home culture and context. Churches can utilize short-term mission trips both to extend the ministry of the church and to provide encouragement for the missionaries. The Yanceys noted that you can use these trips to debrief with your sent ones and provide "down time" where they can relax and be refreshed through a date night or an outing with the team. In their response, the Smiths stressed that "distance is always a challenge for these different aspects of care; however, there should be a greater emphasis on spiritual and emotional evaluation of the missionaries." On-site visits assist in helping churches prioritize this kind of care. I encourage churches either to make on-site visits that are strictly member-care trips in which they encourage, counsel, and even equip (as needed) their missionaries, or to build some of these aspects into a more ministry-focused short-term mission trip, either on the front or back end of their time together.

An often overlooked area of care is the relationship the sending church has with its missionary kid, or "MKs." Trent and Braidi noted that their family has profited from their kids staying connected with their sending church's children's and youth ministries, as they will have a deeper relational bond with that age range. In the same way that advocacy groups within the church adopt the parents, these ministries could adopt certain MKs for which they advocate. They could send care packages and have regular correspondence with the MKs, and, when appropriate, they could also take children and youth on trips to encourage the MKs on the field. Maintaining connections between whole families and the various generations within a church will help the church more meaningfully adopt, pray for, and deeply support their missionaries.

Post-Field Care

If churches excel in on-field care, as reflected by the testimony of those missionaries that were interviewed, then it seems they would also seek to excel in providing care during the reentry and post-field phases, yet this is not always the case. While missionaries expressed gratitude for having a house to stay in when they returned stateside, that is only one aspect of the process of reacclimating into one's home country, culture, and church. Sadly, as Rick Plummer reflected, "The longer one is on the field, the more one becomes forgotten. It is important when they return for stateside assignment (STAS) that they are not ignored as though they don't matter." He highlighted a recent STAS during which a supporting church's senior pastor did not do a faithful job of connecting with him and his family or trying to incorporate them into the life of the congregation.

I saw this reality play out in my own ministry. Whereas I was able to give more focused care and attention in my role on staff, it was challenging for others to know how to engage, especially if the missionaries were not official church partners. It was a unique situation to have missionaries staying in our missions house who were not a part of our missions strategy. Nevertheless, if we use 3 John 5–8 as a template for care, then whenever we have missionaries under our care, even if they are not "official" partners, the church should welcome them in as their own, fill them up, and then send them back out.

The exhortation of Paul in Philippians 2:29–30 to receive the sent one back with all joy and honor is central to post-field care. As the Plummers argued, churches can flesh out this command to celebrate their missionaries by giving them opportunities to speak into the life of the church, share testimonies with the church when on stateside, and find avenues to reincorporate themselves into the ministry of the church once they've returned.

The emphasis a church places on knowing its missionaries, assessing and equipping them, caring for them, and receiving them from the field will have an impact on the physical, emotional, mental, and spiritual health of the missionary. As Trent and Braidi state, "True missionary work always comes with spiritual attacks that can have serious repercussions. These attacks can be on the missionaries' physical, marital, and familial health and are often detrimental to the longevity of the missionaries if they do not have proper support from the local church." Churches would do well to hear and heed the feedback they receive from their sent ones and respond by providing greater care and accountability to those they have sent.

From the Church's Perspective

In assessing the local church's effectiveness in missionary care, I wanted to look beyond the perspective of missionaries and have churches provide self-evaluation as well. I asked three churches of varying sizes to provide feedback on where they see the church excelling and where needs exist for increased or improved missionary care. These three churches were: Antioch Church in Louisville, Kentucky; Grand Avenue Baptist Church in Fort Smith, Arkansas; and The Summit Church in Raleigh-Durham, North Carolina.

These three churches all give credence to the fact that missionary sending and supporting, including the care of its "sent ones," are foundational elements in the DNA of the local church. Bradley Bell, Lead Pastor of Antioch Church, states, "The church is the foundation for sending, all the way from identifying candidates, evaluating, commissioning, and receiving them back into the church. The missionary-church relationship is a reciprocal one; therefore, the church should also have expectations of the missionary." Churches have seen this two-way relationship result in benefits like alleviating missionary attrition. Matt Clark, Member Care Pastor at The Summit Church, affirms, "It is a powerful thing when a missionary knows they are known and loved by their sending church regardless of how 'successful' their ministry is on the field. Open and honest communication both ways in these relationships [is] immensely valuable to the health of the missionaries." These kinds of relationships can be forged between senders and sent ones as members get to know their missionaries deeply.

One way to foster these reciprocal relationships is to establish what we earlier defined as advocacy teams. The three churches I surveyed assign each of their missionary units to an advocate who serves as the primary point of contact and care at the church. As noted by these churches, the level of care they provide varies according to the strength of relationship with the advocate, which demonstrates why the local church, composed of her members, needs to work on building and maintaining a deep relationship of transparency and accountability with its sent ones. Because a strong relationship between advocate and missionary is key to creating a mutually beneficial partnership, churches must be intentional about training their advocacy leaders and setting clear expectations for them. Scott Ward, missions pastor at Grand Avenue Baptist Church, says that some of their partnerships have fallen through the cracks because advocacy leaders have not known what their role and function should be. The relationship was there, but the advocacy leaders weren't clear on how they were to provide care, and the relationship suffered as a result.

A second way these churches give us a healthy example of care is through pastoral care visits. Pastor and author Andy Johnson writes, "churches who send and support missionaries should be willing to invest valuable time and resources simply to 'see how they are.' Visits to love them, listen to them, encourage them through the Bible and prayer may accomplish more than you would imagine."[103] Antioch Church, for example, strives to provide a care visit for each missionary unit once per term.

One area these churches noted that needs greater attention was in provid-

103 Andy Johnson, Missions: How the Local Church Goes Global (Wheaton: Crossway, 2017), 55.

ing care during reentry. Just as the missionaries I surveyed noted, churches are often ill-equipped to receive their sent ones back from the field. Matt Clark of The Summit Church reflected, "we have some things in place, but it is difficult to remain focused and consistent once a goer has returned for good." This oversight may be due to churches not being trained on the front end; at other times, it may occur because so many resources are being applied to on-field care that a church is stretched too thin to provide meaningful care during the reentry phase.

From the Agency's Perspective

Mission agencies were the third group I surveyed in evaluating the church's role in missionary care. The need exists for partnership between the church and the mission agency that is founded on the understanding that the church and the agency have separate and unique aspects of care they can provide. For this study, I surveyed three missionary care personnel from three different mission agencies: Jay Decker[104], Ron and Lisa Jones, and Jamie Haguewood.

Each participant affirmed that many churches are eager to assist in providing care to their sent ones. Decker stated that "depending on what role the sending church wants to play, we are happy to see them take up the primary responsibility for member care in many ways." He noted that while some churches desire to be more proactive in their role of care, others need greater assistance from the mission agency. Although there are many ways in which the responsibilities of missionary care may be shared, Decker affirmed that the local church is the ideal place for the missionary to receive encouragement and counsel: "The sending church usually has a long history with the worker, [whereas] the mission agency has frequently only known them for a few years. When workers require counseling and support, it is ideal that the local church step in and take on some of these functions." Haguewood responded similarly, noting that "relationships from the sending church are by nature more natural and 'organic' than [those] from within the organization." He adds that the potential exists for the relational gap to close between the missionary and the local church when there is greater distance between the missionary and agency. Yet, as we have seen in the missionaries' responses, close bonds between sending church and sent one aren't always a guarantee.

While these agency personnel are encouraged by churches taking a more proactive role in providing care, others emphasized that there is still a need

104 I used a pseudonym for this individual for security purposes.

for churches to be more intentional. The Joneses expressed that, based on their correspondence with the missionaries they oversee, sending churches can provide greater care in the areas of encouragement, counseling, and even logistical support, particularly when it comes to reentry. As we've heard from each group—missionaries, churches, and agencies—the area of reentry care is the most overlooked and in need of greater attention from the church.

The level of care our churches provide is proportionate to their commitment to those they send. Deborah Ford writes that, because missionaries are an extension of the local church body, "pastoral care of cross-cultural missionaries cannot be considered in isolation from congregational care as a whole."[105] The church has a vital role to play in assessing, equipping, caring for, and receiving its sent ones. There are areas in which churches are eager and engaged in care, yet there are other areas that do not receive the attention they deserve. Churches should strive to provide intentional, meaningful care at every stage and give of themselves selflessly and sacrificially so their sent ones can be equipped to participate in their Great Commission call.

105 Ford, 8.

CHAPTER 6

The Role of the Mission Agency in Missionary Care

While the local church has been given the primary charge to care for its sent ones, the mission agency also has a valuable role to play in providing support and care. Unfortunately, these roles are often not clearly defined or understood by churches, agencies, or the missionaries they send. Neal Pirolo discusses the common challenge of distinguishing the functions of the church versus the agency in providing missionary care. He highlights eight areas in which the agency is well-suited to provide care:

1. <u>Recruitment:</u> The agency is best suited to assign the right missionaries to the right team to the right field work in which he or she will be engaged.

2. <u>Pre-field preparation:</u> The agency provides biblical, cross-cultural, linguistic, and orientation training. This preparation also includes the necessary field paperwork.

3. <u>On-field care:</u> The agency provides spiritual, emotional, physical, and social care for the missionary. This responsibility includes coordinating with the sending church to provide adequate care during reentry.

4. <u>Reentry:</u> The agency, in conjunction with the sending church, will provide housing, education, and debriefing opportunities when missionaries are on stateside assignment.

5. <u>Home assignment:</u> The agency will assign certain responsibilities to the missionary for debriefing and recruitment purposes.

6. <u>Conflict management:</u> The agency provides the necessary training for biblical resolution and restoration in times of conflict.

7. <u>Contingency management:</u> The agency provides contingency plans

pertaining to the safety of the missionary and reactions to crisis situations.

8. Crisis-level member care: The agency knows how to step in alongside the sending church to assist in seasons of crisis.[106]

Missions agencies have adequate and experienced staff, financial resources, and the capacity to give meaningful missionary care. It is vital that they take seriously their responsibility to their missionaries and do all they can to ensure their missionaries feel cared for by them. However, as Pirolo highlights, the line needs to be drawn between church and agency so that neither oversteps into the role of the other.[107]

From the Missionary's Perspective

To better understand the roles and effectiveness of missions agencies in providing missionary care, I surveyed the same missionaries, churches, and agencies that provided the responses in chapter 5. Most of the missionaries I surveyed highlighted key ways in which the agency undergirds them with care. Some, like the Smiths, referenced agency personnel who provide varying touchpoints in care, including a regional supervisor, missionary care personnel, and operational staff. The Yanceys and Plummers mentioned other avenues of care, including on-field logistical support, physical provisions (e.g., house, vehicle), and safety and security oversight. While some churches may have the resources and expertise to provide these practical aspects of care, many churches do not and should look to missions agencies to meet these needs.

In addition to practical needs, the missionaries also spoke of personal touch points they receive in missionary care from their agency. Susannah Brock said that in her first years on the field, she had the opportunity to meet regularly with a mentor assigned by the agency. Missionaries like the Smiths and the Browns also benefit from regular training and equipping. Times of crisis provide opportunities for an agency with skilled and licensed counselors to provide necessary care. Trent and Braidi recalled interactions with agency-appointed counselors when dealing with assimilation issues with one of their children on the field. As I mentioned in an earlier chapter, this is an area where the church can collaborate and coordinate with the agency. There is certainly a role the agency needs to play, but because sent ones are still under the spiritual oversight of local churches, the leadership of that church

---

106 Neal Pirolo, "Four Levels of Missionary Care: Part Three," Upstream Collective, 15 May 2019, http://www.theupstreamcollective.org/post/four-levels-of-missionary-care-part-three.

107 Ibid.

should have opportunities to help guide that counseling.

While the responses of the missionaries reflect that their mission agencies have provided ample care, these organizations cannot and should not provide all the care an individual or family needs. Expecting them to do so puts too much weight on the agency and undermines the role of the local church. Eric Wright comments, "The perception that a mission agency has the resources to completely care for a missionary is [an illusion]."[108] Sometimes, agencies can overstep their bounds and exert too much authority over their missionaries. Trent and Braidi Brown attest to how their mission agency often does not understand the rigors of missionary life and functions in more of a policing than a pastoral role. They said that this mindset becomes clear when the agency chooses to bring a missionary home rather than deal with the issues at hand. They further stated, "The member care department has too much power in our agency and often does not have the best interest of the missionary, family, or strategy in mind when making decisions." Examples like this illustrate the importance of maintaining an ongoing conversation and relationship between sending churches, agencies, and the missionaries they send.

From the Church's Perspective

As the primary caregiver alongside the mission agency, the church must maintain a strong relationship with the agencies that oversee their sent ones. I surveyed the same three churches from chapter 5 to better understand their working relationships with various mission entities and what they perceive are the agencies' strengths and weaknesses.

Grand Avenue Baptist Church partners primarily with the two Southern Baptist Convention missions entities: the North American Mission Board (NAMB) and the International Mission Board (IMB). Because of their strong denominational ties, the church rarely ventures beyond these entities in their mission partnerships. Pastor Scott Ward believes their church is able to complement the care their missionaries receive from these agencies, and because the IMB, in particular, does not set many expectations on the local church to provide care, any care the church does provide serves as a bonus to the missionary.

The Summit Church also partners with the NAMB and the IMB and works alongside them to provide care. For missionaries going with the IMB, for example, both Summit and the IMB provide a joint assessment in

108 Wright, 232.

pre-field care and collectively provide ongoing care while a missionary unit is on the field. Beyond these partnerships, Pastor Matt Clark said that Summit also works with other agencies that align with the church's mission, vision, and church-planting focus. "We value these organizations' commitment to equip and care for those partnering with them as well as their commitment to working as a part of a missionary team."

From the Agency's Perspective

Just as the church should reflect on its ability to provide adequate care for missionaries, the agency also needs to evaluate its effectiveness in this area. Here is a brief snapshot of three agencies[109] I corresponded with: "Agency G" is a non-denominational mission agency that began as an extension of the ministry of Ethnos 360 but has served as its own entity since 2012. They have 140 missionaries representing sixty-four sending churches serving under their watch care. Jay Decker, who serves as their missionary care consultant, highlights the various areas of care that they provide for their missionaries, including culture, language and translation consultants, church relations, logistics support, and business consulting. "Agency R," which has been operating since 2013, has fifty missionary units on the field and serves alongside forty-five sending churches. Jamie Haguewood, missionary care specialist for Agency R, describes their care as providing general counsel and encouragement to their missionaries. "Agency I," which has been sending and supporting missionaries for 175 years, is the longest-standing mission agency I surveyed and has 3,667 missionaries serving under its care. Ron and Lisa Jones are regional missionary care consultants in the Central and South America region and highlighted the clinical and pastoral care they give to their missionaries.

Although the relationship between the sending church and the mission agency has not always been clear, the mission agency representatives noted that churches have begun to take a more active approach in providing care to their missionaries. Decker states, "Historically, probably because of the limited communication technology of the time, churches grew accustomed to taking a very 'hands off' approach to the actual ministry of missionaries overseas and entrusted all leadership and accountability to the agency." While the church is becoming more active in providing care, there are still areas in which the agency is best suited to give particular oversight.

Haguewood, for example, believes agencies are well-equipped to provide soul care that addresses the amount of stress missionaries endure in their

---

109 I used abbreviations for the agencies instead of their actual names.

field of service. On-Field stressors abound, and mission agencies often have a better handle on the specifics of how to address those. The Joneses appreciate that their mission agency has certain benchmarks and expectations regarding their job performance and that it can assess and evaluate their service more adequately than their sending church can. They also appreciate the specific field resourcing with which the agency undergirds its missionaries, since most churches do not have the sufficient knowledge or experience to equip their sent ones for life overseas. The agency has experts in the field, focused resources, and cross-cultural competencies that allow them to serve missionaries in ways most churches cannot; however, they, like the church, must know their limits, and there may be instances where they need to defer to the church's care, involvement, and leadership. As the church and mission agency both understand their unique roles and the resources they can provide in missionary care, a healthy partnership between them and the missionaries they serve can be lived out.

CHAPTER 7

The Partnership between the Local Church and the Mission Agency

Both the local church and the mission agency have distinct roles in caring for missionaries. Both entities must carry out their unique responsibilities to ensure that adequate care is established and maintained. Ultimately, the church and agency exist to serve the missionary. Thomas Hale and Gene Daniels write, "There is no reason for a divorce between church and mission agency; let them carry on their respective tasks, administratively separate, but in close harmony and cooperation."[110] This kind of cooperation is ideal, but, unfortunately, it has not been the norm. Kelly O'Donnell highlights that much of the responsibility in preparation and ongoing care has been placed in the hands of the agency, leaving the church in a narrowed role of praying and paying with only occasional opportunity to meet tangible needs. This limiting of the local church's role in sending has resulted in a competitive spirit between the two entities. In light of this, O'Donnell states, "It is imperative that the local church play a larger role in world missions, particularly in the care of the missionaries they send out."[111] Sending churches and mission agencies must make an effort and create a plan for working together as they establish trust and partnership. This kind of relationship requires understanding where there are both gaps in care and opportunities to partner.

Potential Gaps in Partnership between the Church and Agency

Gaps in missionary care between the church and agency often lead to disappointment and frustration in their missionaries, which can result

110 Hale and Daniels, 158–59.
111 O'Donnell, *Missionary Care*, 299, 303.

in them experiencing a sense of isolation, higher stress, and even burnout. David Wilson notes, "By minding the gaps in missionary care, the church can create a system of proactive care which will ensure lasting engagement of both the local church and the agency in the lives of our beloved missionaries."[112] While gaps may exist in many areas, this section will focus on improving care for three categories of missionaries: singles, couples, and missionary kids.

Singles

One often-overlooked segment of the missionary force is singles. Christians can trace the history of missions and observe where key singles like Lottie Moon, Mary Slessor, and Amy Carmichael were instrumental in the proclamation of the gospel message. In regard to caring for singles, Rob Hay remarks that "singles need special pastoral care. They need to know and understand the reality of life on the field, both the dangers and the challenges. They need help integrating into teams, where they can contribute and be respected as partners in ministry."[113] Single missionaries can attest to this desire for care, concern, and community on a team: Susannah Brock writes,

There are a lot of resources on caring for families on the field, but there aren't many on caring for singles. While the first few years can be lonely for anyone, I think it can be especially so for a single who is having to pack, move, transition, learn how to do everyday tasks in a new language and culture, make friends, and do so many other things on their own. While the job of caring for singles in these ways falls primarily on the local team, both the sending church and the agency should be aware of the unique challenges of being on the field as a single and offer support as needed.

As missionary teams, churches, and agencies work to mobilize college students or young adults for missionary service, they need to look for strategic roles that singles can fill. Both in my capacity as missions pastor and in my current mobilization role, I am mindful of the need to encourage churches to help singles consider opportunities like gap years, student exchange programs, and the IMB Journeyman program, to name a few. The church also needs to encourage single sent ones who may feel as though being unmarried will hinder their capacity for missionary service and recognize the opportunity to provide them with additional community through the church.

Couples

I also considered the gap in care given to married couples on the field.

112 Wilson, 8.
113 Hay, 154.

Marriage is marked by both highs and lows and a host of relational stressors, all of which are intensified by life on the mission field. It is crucial that the local church speak into the life of their married missionary couples and seek to exhort them, encourage them, and enhance their relationship. The church must speak into couples' lives in key areas as well as provide regular check-ups through consistent communication on the field and when couples return home.

When I served as missions pastor, I would work with our other pastoral staff to set up times for our missionaries who were stateside to do a "marriage check-up," which would include a marriage enrichment session. We would have a one-on-one counseling session with the couple to debrief, then we would go through an online enrichment tool with them, which helped pinpoint areas of strength and areas for growth in their marriage. Our staff would then set up subsequent meetings to work through those results and counsel in those areas. These check-ups aided couples in reflecting on the ways they could uniquely serve one another on the field, and they often revealed ways in which life on the field had caused them to put ministry before marriage. Churches can also send their couples to marriage conferences and give them date nights, both when they're on the field (by sending money for a babysitter or giving couples a night out during short-term trips) and when they're stateside. Churches must understand how important a healthy marriage is to long-term missionary service and help their missionaries' marriages stay healthy. If the marriage is suffering, then the ministry and missionary service will suffer as well.

Missionary Kids

Providing meaningful care to children of missionaries, or *missionary kids* (MKs), is an often-overlooked aspect of missionary care. MKs represent a subset of what are called *third culture kids* (TCKs), which authors David Pollock, Ruth Van Reken, and Michael Pollock define as "a person who has spent a significant part of his or her developmental years outside the parents' culture. The TCK frequently builds relationships to all of the cultures while not having full ownership of any."[114] In her research of TCKs, Tanya Crossman found that "62 percent of TCKs born after 1985 said that 'feeling in between' was a significant part of their childhood experience."[115] Crossman identified other common traits and characteristics of TCKs, including being misunderstood by family and friends.[116] According to former missionary kid

114 David C. Pollock, Ruth E. Van Reken, and Michael V. Pollock, *Third Culture Kids: Growing Up Among Worlds*, 3rd ed. (Boston, MA: Nicholas Brealey, 2017), 16.
115 Tanya Crossman, Misunderstood: *The Impact of Growing Up Overseas in the 21st Century* (Greater London, UK: Summertime Publishing, 2016), 4.
116 Ibid., 23–24, 27.

Gregg Turner, what separates MKs from TCKs is that MKs "moved because God called [their] parents,"[117] whereas TCKs moved for their parents' jobs in the business world or military.

Whatever led to their move across cultures—be it missions or military—a TCK's life is marked by two constants: coming and going. Pollock, Van Reken, and Pollock write, "Being raised in a genuinely cross-culture world, TCKs actually live in different cultural worlds as they travel back and forth between their passport and host cultures ... being raised in a highly mobile world, they are either coming or going."[118] They further highlight the identity crisis TCKs go through in having to answer the questions, *Who am I? Where do I belong? and Where Is Home?* Because of the transient nature of a TCK's life, these questions are often difficult to answer.[119]

It is important for TCKs to establish a sense of identity, because "when TCKs come to understand they have their place of belonging, they can more easily find new ways to name how they belong to the other cultures and places of their lives as well."[120] By understanding where they belong and who they are, a TCK's identity can be "both/and" with their present and passport cultures rather than "either/or," which aids the flow of maturation a child goes through on the field.[121] This truth seems important for the church to understand, so that as communication with missionaries and their children takes place, the church can better listen for and respond to the issues of uncertainty or frustrations MKs experience. [122]

I was encouraged to see members of our church give their kids opportunities to invest in the lives of MKs. They did this both by bringing their children with them on short-term trips and by keeping in constant communication with MKs on the field. Just as the missionaries were refreshed by visits with adults from their sending church, the kids were elated to have other kids from their "home" culture and church in their midst. Taking these opportunities can also be a form of missions education and a mobilization tool to stir a missionary desire in the lives of younger generations. A man from our church named Mike took each of his children on a short-term trip to the same partner on the field once they reached early adolescence. These trips gave Mike and his kids a chance to bond, deepened the partnership between

---

117 Gregg Turner, Jr., "Are the Kids Alright? An Introduction to Missionary Kids and the Sending Church," *Reaching & Teaching Blog*, 19 January 2021, https://rtim.org/are-the-kids-alright/.

118 Pollock, Van Reken, and Pollock, 18.

119 Ibid., 55, 188.

120 Ibid., 68.

121 Ibid., 217.

122 Neal Pirolo, *The Reentry Team: Caring for Your Returning Missionaries* (San Diego, CA: Emmaus Road International, Inc., 2000), 163.

this family and the missionaries they had been faithfully praying for, and exposed Mike's kids to the nations.

Avenues to Partnership between the Church and Agency

Although they each have different roles, the local church and mission agency need to find a way forward for supporting one another and working together to care for the missionaries they have sent out. Neal Pirolo insists that "The church cannot—must not—leave the responsibilities of missions to the care of mission agencies. There must be a cooperative relationship— the church doing the things it can do best and the agency doing its part."[123] Steve Beirn and George Murray believe missionary care should be a matter of teamwork, rather than a siloed approach. They write,

> The individual seeking to follow Christ's command to make disciples of all nations will learn how vital it is to commit to and be sent out by a local church. That local church will be better equipped to guide and support that individual, and mission agencies will be able to support the local church leadership by casting vision and providing additional global ministry expertise.[124]

They further highlight that if the church sends and the agency serves as a facilitator, then "It makes sense to bring these parties together for productive ministry. It is important to know that 'going it alone' often results in the duplication of efforts and a lack of expertise."[125] As each party puts forth effort to cooperate, all can excel in the areas in which they are best equipped to shepherd sent ones. As we discovered in chapter 6, many agencies welcome the prospect of churches being more heavily involved in the missionary care process and recognize the church's role and responsibility in shepherding their own missionary members.

One essential to a meaningful partnership between sending church and agency is maintaining clear communication. Rob Hay explains, "Ideally, there should be free flowing communication between staff, missionaries, and leadership as well as structured processes for input into the agency leadership and direction."[126] Local churches need to inquire about agency leadership

123 Ibid., 286.
124 Beirn and Murray, 20.
125 Ibid., 109.
126 Hay, 242.

and resources to know where they need to take the lead and fill gaps. Areas to assess could include health, safety, security, and educational needs.[127] Wilson writes, "The church needs to understand its role of caring for the individual while at the same time understanding that the agency has much larger issues on the field to consider . . . [both] can pair together and share resources without dividing up roles and responsibilities."[128] As the church and agency communicate and work collaboratively, a customized care plan can be developed for each missionary they send.

I appreciated being able to work collaboratively with agency representatives and future field team leaders as we were preparing a young couple and a newly graduated college student for the field. The couple desired to serve two years with one of our church's long-term partners. We were able to have the reins during the assessment and initial interview process, and it was through this process that we were able to collaborate with the agency representatives to review information regarding the couple's health and qualifications. While this couple did not end up on the mission field, we had already started to establish a care plan for them on the front end of the process.

The postgraduate, who served a Journeyman term, benefited from the church and agency's partnership as we worked through some areas that needed to be addressed prior to recommending him for the next stage in the process. As of the writing of this book, he is set to begin his two-year term, and he has grown in spiritual maturity as a result of the church and agency working hand-in-hand.

As church and agency communicate throughout the sending process, some disagreements will likely arise. However, "when both parties are humble and honest, a plan for effective and sustainable vitality in the missionary is possible. In general, the agency has the final say on matters of acceptance, training, and legal ramifications."[129] As the agency serves the church in overseeing these larger facets of care, a more biblical picture of unity results.[130]

A second important mark of a strong partnership between church and agency is the church knowing what kind of church it is and what role it will play in caring for its missionaries. Wilson distinguishes between a "sending church" and a "supporting church":

> We define a "sending church" as the one which takes full responsibility of a missionary on behalf of the agency for

127 Wilson, 91–93.
128 Ibid., 96.
129 Hay, 98.
130 Wilson, 373.

the purposes of commissioning, missionary care, and over-all development in partnership with the agency. "Support-ing Church" is a church that may provide funding, but does not "co-sign" for the missionary with the agency.[131]

Keeping these kinds of distinctions in mind will help the church and agency build and maintain greater accountability. Deborah Ford outlines some areas where the church and agency are held accountable to one another. For example, the agency should keep the local church informed when they make changes in assignment or shifts in status, and the local church should communicate with the agency about the personal touchpoints of advocacy they are making with their missionaries on the field.[132] By communicating transparently and defining roles clearly, the church and agency can hold each other accountable to their areas of responsibility.

A third important mark of a strong partnership pertains to advocacy. As Kelly O'Donnell emphasizes, "Preventative pastoral care of field mission-aries is one way in which [mission agencies] are addressing the increasing-ly complex spiritual, emotional, and psychological needs of their mission-aries."[133] Local churches can also provide pastoral care by assigning church leadership or key members to care for their missionaries. Wilson remarks that "having a care team of people who won't over interpret their struggles will increase a missionary's openness . . . but having a clear [agreement estab-lished] will keep things confidential, making it even more likely that this type of communication will take place."[134] Pirolo highlights four levels at which both the church and agency can come alongside the missionary. First, the church can help "the missionary [solicit] a team of caregivers, thus build-ing ownership in the process. Second, the mission agency can provide devel-opmental training in advocacy. Third, the church and her leadership deter-mine what areas of care are needed. Finally, this team is released to fulfill their missionary care role."[135] Partnership through advocacy has the benefit of closing potential gaps in care in these areas.[136]

A fourth and final opportunity for partnership comes during the reentry stage. As Pirolo states, "The reentry time in the life of the missionary remains shrouded in ignorance. I believe the mission agency is more aware of the problems of reentry [than the church], but [often they] do not have the staff

---

131 Ibid., 56. Wilson recognizes that some churches are positioned to serve as sending churches, whereas others are better suited to take the role of a supporting church.

132 Ford, 8.

133 O'Donnell, *Missionary Care*, 31.

134 Wilson, 25.

135 Pirolo, *The Reentry Team*, 247.

136 Wilson, 93-94.

to deal with the issues."[137] He further points out that the church often has the relationship but not the knowledge, hence the need for church and agency to work together. [138] If churches can communicate with their missionaries and seek to understand their needs prior to their return stateside, then it would help ease the reentry process. This might include helping them in the areas of debriefing, counseling, conflict resolution, marriage evaluation, or even simply providing opportunities for rest and physical provisions (housing, transportation, etc.).

Recognizing gaps in care and looking for onramps to partnership must occur to establish healthy levels of communication, accountability, advocacy, and retention between the missionary, church, and agency. As Jay Decker (missionary care consultant from chapter 6) notes, "I think this is a positive development, and as the level of partnership between churches, those they send out, and agencies continues to grow, it will be a positive thing for the advancement of the kingdom around the world." A posture of humility, a desire for partnership, and a shared commitment to those they've sent will help churches and agencies work together to provide faithful, meaningful missionary care.

137 Pirolo, *The Reentry Team*, 17.
138 Ibid., 19.

CHAPTER 8

Models of Churches Providing Missionary Care

While the need exists for all sending churches to take greater owner-ship in missionary care, some churches will take on the distinct and intentional identity of being a "Missionary Care Sending Church." Mike Ironside defines these churches by stating, "The Missionary Care Sending Church desires to make those they send feel loved, cared for, and accountable to what they are sent to accomplish. They are less concerned with a particular strategy for sending and are, instead, focused on how those who are sent are doing personally and how connected they feel to the church."[139] In other words, these churches put a higher emphasis on the character, competencies, and capacity of the individuals they send than they do on the place or the project with which they want to build a mission partnership. Ironside further states that "to be a great Missionary Care Sending Church, the leadership will want to create opportunities for those who are interested in global missions to be proactively mentored prior to going overseas."[140] This kind of assessment process would address the physical, emotional, spiritual, and relational health of those considering being sent.

With this kind of sending church in mind, I surveyed three churches of varying sizes to assess the type of missionary care they provide.

Antioch Church

Antioch Church in Louisville, Kentucky, is affiliated with the Southern Baptist Convention (SBC) and has a total membership of 120. Currently, they do not have a staff member dedicated to overseeing their missions efforts. Bradley Bell, Lead Pastor of Antioch, describes their framework for sending

---

139 Mike Ironside, "Four Types of Sending Churches: Missionary Care Sending Church," Upstream Collective, 7 May 2021, https://www.theupstreamcollective.org/post/four-types-of-sending-churches-missionary-care-sending-church.

140 Ibid.

missionaries by grounding their strategy in the context of the local church. He says, "The church is the foundation for sending, all the way from identifying candidates, evaluating, commissioning, and receiving them back into the church. The missionary-church relationship is a reciprocal one, meaning the church should have expectations for the missionary as well." Antioch has shown itself to be a faithful sending church, as they have equipped and released six families to the mission field during the last five years.

Antioch, though small, values sending missionaries and supporting them throughout their time on the field. They organize their missionary care primarily through missionary advocates, which are teams responsible for providing care for missionaries. One person on each team serves as the point of contact for the missionary, but the entire team assists in different ways to facilitate missionary care. Bell says the level of care varies depending on the strength of the relationship between the advocacy team and their missionary. These teams strive not only to provide care from afar but also to take one care trip each year to visit that missionary unit on the field. Even though it is a smaller church, Antioch strategically sends and adequately supports its missionaries.

Grand Avenue Baptist Church

Like Antioch, Grand Avenue Baptist Church is affiliated with the SBC. Their membership totals 2,000 and they have a paid, full-time missions pastor in Scott Ward. He describes their sending strategy in this way: "We believe the Great Commission is a general call to all believers; therefore, we attempt to mobilize and send everyone to all the people groups through education and missions experiences, such as short-term mission trips." Grand Avenue's sending heartbeat has led them to send five missionary units to the field in as many years.

Grand Avenue leans heavily upon the IMB and works alongside it to provide missionary care. They also send missionary care teams to visit their partners on an annual basis and have kept their church engaged through virtual mission trips during the COVID-19 pandemic. Similar to Antioch Church, Grand Avenue has built advocacy teams for each of their mission partnerships, and Ward says the strength of these teams has varied based on the depth of relationship between the advocates and their missionaries. He also highlighted that they emphasize helping their missionary couples maintain healthy marriages and have even hosted marriage retreats on the field.

The Summit Church

The Summit Church is also part of the SBC and has 7,047 members. Summit employs a mission team with specific staff dedicated to missionary care. Matt Clark, Pastor of Missionary Care at Summit, says their sending strategy is centered on Matthew 28:16–20 and emphasizes going, evangelizing, and disciple-making. As a larger church, they have the capacity and resources to send a larger contingency of their membership to the field. They leverage being strategically located near large universities in the Raleigh-Durham area and seek to mobilize college students and young professionals. Over the last five years, they have sent fifty-two families, eight couples, forty-one singles, and four retired members to the mission field.

Summit has a robust equipping and care strategy for their missionaries. They have specific pre-field training for members who are going as missionaries, and they train missionary care advocates in providing care to their sent ones. Their care strategy centers on having monthly touchpoints with mission partners, equipping missionaries to budget for the field, counseling in cross-cultural issues, and sending missionary care teams. Summit's missionary care teams utilize a group of retired or near-retired members called The SENT network. Because these members are "empty nesters," they have a greater capacity than others in the church to provide care on the field for their missionaries. In addition to providing on-field care, the SENT network also facilitates reentry care.

Although these churches differ in size, setting, and resources, they each provide an example of what it means to be a Missionary Care Sending Church. Some have staff dedicated to overseeing mission efforts, while others do not. However, all engage a broad scope of their membership in the care of missionaries. As advocacy teams are formed, care trips are taken, and reentry strategies are implemented, relationships are strengthened as sending churches provide shepherding care that fosters staying power for their sent ones.

CHAPTER 9

Best Practices for Missionary Retention

So far, we have defined missionary care and discussed the value of such care; surveyed the roles of the church and agency as understood from the field, church, and agency viewpoints; addressed gaps in and avenues for partnership between the church and agency; and reviewed models for missionary care. Now we will conclude this section by looking at key markers in missionary care that foster missionary retention. These markers span the areas of pre-field, on-field, and post-field care, as all three must happen to build up, send out, and support strong missionaries.

Pre-Field Missionary Care

As highlighted in the responses of the missionaries I surveyed, pre-field assessment and equipping is often lacking in a church's sending strategy. Neal Pirolo writes that "the first issue at this (pre-field) level is the identifying and nurturing of a prospective missionary. This will probably begin long before that person realizes a personal call."[141] Steve Beirn and George Murray concur that this assessment and equipping time is a key stage in a missionary's preparation. They state, "A better ministry fit makes a better missionary."[142] Churches need to work alongside their missionaries and in partnership with the agency during the pre-field stage to find the right ministry fit, which will aid in missionary retention on the field and strengthen the partnership among entities.

Assessment

As churches observe and evaluate a candidate's readiness, they have the opportunity to note areas where they can extend care and establish metrics by which to do so. Earlier, I referenced two different missionary units that

141 Pirolo, "Four Levels of Missionary Care: Part One."
142 Beirn and Murray, 92.

our church was able to assist in the assessment process alongside the mission agency. For the couple we sent, this provided a great opportunity to recognize areas in their marriage that needed to be strengthened through counseling. For the recent college graduate, we discovered areas of purity and discipleship that needed to be addressed and strengthened. Mike Ironside writes, "church leaders should be able to observe these members engaging in missional living and cross-cultural missions. Their capacity to excel at these things is a key marker of whether or not they should go overseas."[143] Other markers include spiritual disciplines, a spirit of humility, teamwork, faith, persistence, and flexibility.[144] Even though the assessment should be led by key church leadership, it is a whole-church process. As a missionary candidate is both known in relationship and their gifts are evidenced by a good cross-section of the church, the church can have collective confidence in that candidate's call, character, and competency.

Churches can assess readiness by crafting a personal development plan through their pre-field correspondence with the mission agency and field personnel. Ironside encourages churches to focus on the spiritual health, emotional health, relational health, ministry skills, and personal health of the candidate as they develop this plan.[145] Churches should measure these areas in the pre-field assessment and use them as an ongoing metric for health and sustainability in the missionary's life on the field. Using this development plan can help gauge if the missionary has zeal, wisdom, and experience, all of which are necessary to endure the challenges associated with cross-cultural missions. Eric Wright exhorts, "Zeal and youthful energy are needed, but they must be harnessed by the maturity and approach that is found in those who have already endured problems, trials, challenges, and disappointments with a measure of stability."[146]

Seasons of trial will come, and it is during those seasons that the inward call of God must keep a missionary tethered to the field. That call must be sensed inwardly and affirmed outwardly by the sending church. Asking probing and open-ended questions in the assessment process about how a candidate has had to work through a challenging situation or a relational conflict will shed light on how they might handle potential cross-cultural challenges or team conflict. Providing opportunities for short-term missions work will also allow the candidate to exercise their character and skill in a cross-cultural context. Thomas Hale and Gene Daniels write, "The sending church must

143 Mike Ironside, "The Sending Pipeline: From US Senders or Potential Goers to Committed Goers," Upstream Collective, 27 September 2021, https://www.theupstreamcollective.org/post/the-sending-pipeline-from-us-senders-or-potential-goers-to-committed-goers.
144 Wright, 190; and Hay, 90.
145 Ironside, "The Sending Pipeline."
146 Wright, 185.

share in this call—they have the duty to examine the call and modify it as necessary. And together with the missionary, they will need to evaluate the results of the call. An isolated call in itself never justifies a missionary's activities."[147] By affirming a missionary's call, the church makes itself accountable for providing the care needed within that individual's life and ministry.

Training

As the church assesses and affirms missionaries, they then need to train and equip them for life on the mission field. They should not silo the training but, instead, seek to make it a whole-church effort to equip both goers and senders adequately.[148] An awareness of the spiritual battles missionaries face ought to spur churches to ensure and affirm a clear call and, in connection with mission agencies, provide thorough training. Wright exhorts, "Missionaries should be among our best-trained professionals. They represent Christ in new churches. They must know the Scriptures thoroughly, as well as have facility in missionary methodology."[149] Wright presents the local church as the incubator for training in the Bible and doctrine.[150] Eckhard Schnabel writes that such training is reflected in the Scriptures (namely, 1 Timothy and Titus) and "distinguished in four areas of character, commitment, competency, and culture."[151] One is able to determine readiness by observing a candidate's life and doctrine, as well as the faithfulness and fruit of their current ministry, especially as it relates to their engagement with other cultures. As I've mentioned previously, missions training courses, reading groups, and local and global missional opportunities aid in this season of training.

This training must involve not only intake but also output. Rob Hay notes, "A high correlation for retention was found for selecting people who had a chance to 'practice' ministry in their local church."[152] Missionary candidates, in partnership with the church, can clearly see their strengths and weaknesses as they engage in pre-field training. As in any field, the better one is prepared, the better they will perform and the longer they will serve.[153] Considering how one might not only survive but also thrive on the field can occur through a pre-field visit. This type of visit allows a candidate to evaluate their gifts and talents and whether the context matches their person-

147 Hale and Daniels, 22.

148 Ford, 6.

149 Wright, 189.

150 Ibid., 228.

151 Eckhard J. Schnabel, *Paul the Missionary: The Realities, Strategies and Methods* (Downers Grove: IL, 2008), 390.

152 Hay, 72.

153 Ibid., 109.

al calling as they interact with the existing team in that location and assess their competency for the job requirements.[154] It also provides the opportunity for them to receive feedback from the field as they do their own self-assessment. This assessment and equipping in discerning calling, developing skills, and deciphering location are needed components for both the prospective missionary and sending church to mark out steps to the field and establish a plan for care on the field.

On-Field Missionary Care

As churches develop solid pre-field assessment, training, and care plans, it should naturally transition to healthy on-field missionary care. Churches shouldn't just limit the scope of their on-field care to logistics but should also identify the areas and unique life stages to which the entire church can provide particular care. Two areas of care that deserve greater emphasis are prayer and advocacy teams; two groups that need particular focus are women and missionary kids.[155]

Prayer

Those in the church who cannot go to the field for various reasons can still provide strategic care through prayer. David Wilson notes, "Your missionaries need to know you are praying for them and what you are asking the Lord to do. That is a sincere form of encouragement and a much-appreciated reason to let them know they are not forgotten."[156] Bill Cook and Chuck Lawless express concern that believers often become more reactive than proactive in praying for missionaries. They write, "They pray only when they hear a concern from a missionary on the field—and sometimes praying only begins after the enemy has already won a battle in a missionary's life . . . cover the missionary in prayer before the battle begins, while the battle is ongoing, and after the battle is over."[157] Prayer must be a weapon that churches continually wield. One of the commitments to partnership we asked our missionaries to agree to was providing regular prayer updates. This allowed us to stay connected on ways to intercede for them, their families, and their ministry.

Praying for missionaries not only provides individual care, but it also builds communal bonds across the life of the church. Finding ways to include

154 Hay, 151.

155 These two groups were noted as particular gaps in care and, therefore, emphasized here as those who need particular on-field care.

156 Wilson, 68.

157 Cook and Lawless, 279.

prayer for the nations across the church's various ministries helps build awareness and increase advocacy for missionaries. Whether it's by praying for missionaries in the service, highlighting them through weekly newsletters, including them in your member directory, or having them share with the church when stateside, thinking strategically about prayer for sent ones is crucial. Wilson says, "Praying with others can provide accountability, mutual encouragement, and opportunities to learn more about the missionaries and their work."[158] Wilson advocates for establishing missionary prayer groups to assist in providing personal connection and involvement between members and missionaries on the field.

Advocacy Teams

The missionaries and churches I researched all attested that having a strong contingency of the church as rope-holders helps to bolster the morale of missionaries on the field. Neal Pirolo asserts that "no cross-cultural worker should leave home without a strong, integrated, educated, knowledgeable, active team of people who have committed themselves to the work of serving as senders."[159] Just as the church at Philippi (Phil 4:15) did for Paul by entering into a partnership with him in his times of joy and of loneliness, and by way of exhortation and challenge, churches provide a system of ongoing support by creating advocacy care teams.[160]

Advocacy care teams can include a small group of members assigned to a missionary who have covenanted and committed to ongoing care. Members of these teams get to know their missionaries, their stories, their heart for ministry, and even their successes and disappointments on the field.[161] I recall an Adult Bible Fellowship class that adopted one of our church's missionary families. This class regularly prayed for that family, corresponded with them, and sent members of that class to serve with them through ministry and missionary care trips. The depth of the partnership grew because the depth and breadth of the relationship grew through real and tangible expressions of support and care. Neal Pirolo comments, "Get involved in their lives on the field . . . express interest in the concerns of their hearts . . . ask questions about their lives . . . and respond to communication with you."[162] Advocacy teams and pastoral leadership can also serve their missionaries by going on care trips. Mission strategist Rob Hay describes the purpose of these trips as being strictly for missionary care and not for "ministry." The spirit of the team serving should be one of mercy and pastoring. Churches can use these

158 Wilson, 70.
159 Pirolo, *Serving as Senders Today*, 12.
160 Ibid., 29.
161 Wilson, 69, 77.
162 Pirolo, *Serving as Senders Today*, 124.

trips to bless missionaries with tangible gifts and resources and should allot plenty of time for listening and praying.[163] Advocacy teams can build that culture of care, be a trusted source of communication to and from the field, and propel some to move from being senders to sent ones.

Care to Women

As I noted above, single women often experience a gap in missionary care. This gap frequently takes place in-country as an existing team seeks to find the right fit for a woman, but it also may occur while they are on the field. Anna Daub presents practical advice for improving this care, beginning with sending single females a care package. The church should get to know this individual's needs and include her family in that process.[164] The church also should have significant conversations about security. Daub writes, "Many women feel vulnerable in their own culture and context and a new context only amplifies the vulnerability . . . talk to her about those feelings . . . some women move to places that don't just feel unsafe—they are unsafe . . . learn to be a listener [in those situations]."[165] As women experience a lack of connectivity and heightened vulnerability, feelings of loneliness will tend to arise. In these moments, the church ought to show compassion while also helping singles see the opportunities afforded them—such as having more capacity for ministry and the potential for more connectivity with others—by their unique life-stage as a single.[166] Our church sent a single female to the mission field in a mid-term opportunity and then for long-term service. We were in regular correspondence with her team before she left to get a sense for how she would fit in with them. We maintained ongoing communication to evaluate how her gifts were being utilized and how we could support her emotionally and spiritually, and we were mindful of her unique needs as she returned from the field.

Missionary Kids

Much like single women, missionary kids (MKs) often are an underserved group in the missionary care efforts of local churches. The transient life of an MK can produce feelings of isolation, identity confusion, and a lack of belonging, and the church should be aware of these struggles and seek to care well for these young sent ones in ways that address the unique challenges of being an MK. Gregg Turner Jr., a former MK, notes that believers can

163 Hay, 159–60.

164 Anna Daub, "How the Local Church Can Support Single Women on the Mission Field," Upstream Collective, 9 March 2020, https://www.theupstreamcollective.org/post/how-the-local-church-can-support-single-women-on-the-mission-field/.

165 Ibid.

166 Ibid.

pray specifically for MKs in the areas of language, schooling, friendships, and discipleship. He warns, however, that churches must take care to avoid labeling MKs as missionaries themselves. Some MKs are not Christians, so it is valuable to ask them about their beliefs, and if they do believe, to strengthen them in core doctrines of the faith.[167]

Long-term commitments are crucial to forging long-lasting relationships with missionaries and their children. The Adult Bible Fellowship class noted above took the initiative to fold their kids into the partnering process. These kids wrote letters and emails and held regular Zoom calls with the MKs. They also were able to travel on more than one occasion with their parents to bless the MKs on the field. What encouragement this provided, not only for the missionaries, but also for their children, and the sending church was blessed in return by the deepened relationship with their missionary family. As sending churches listen to their MKs, recognize their youth, and adapt to their interests by entering their world and culture, they can care well for their missionaries by caring for their families.[168]

Post-Field Missionary Care

Post-field care can be the most challenging care for churches to provide. Missionaries come home for numerous reasons—scheduled visits, life events, abrupt endings or retirements—and just as the church needs to be the launching pad for its missionaries, it also needs to be the place to which its missionaries can safely and confidently return.[169] Neal Pirolo writes, "Not only is it crucial for a missionary to have a home church from which to be sent, but . . . upon reentry, it should be their first stop."[170] He argues that if a church has buy-in with sending a missionary to the field and supporting them on the field, then they should also receive that missionary home from the field in a hospitable way. "If you are diligent in properly sending out your missionary, you also need to carve out the time and energy to bring him home safely," says Pirolo.[171] Zach Bradley notes that just as ambassadors represent a foreign country, so missionaries represent an eternal king; therefore, while missionaries "are not of greater value to the body of Christ [than other members] . . . they are worthy of a family-like reunion, and ongoing shepherding through the grueling reentry process."[172] As the missionaries I interviewed believe, it is not that churches do not want to assist but, rather, that they often are unin-

167 Turner, Jr.
168 Ibid.
169 Pirolo, *The Reentry Team*, 242.
170 Ibid., 25.
171 Ibid., 26.
172 Bradley, McCrary, Calfee, and Jansen, ch. 7, "Welcoming Sent Ones."

formed or ill-equipped in caring for returning missionaries.

Reverse Culture Shock

Churches sometimes have a hard time relating to missionaries during the reentry phase because of the reverse culture shock[173] missionaries often experience. Reverse culture shock is a normal experience for returning sent ones, and it can often be more jarring than the shock of entering a new culture for the first time. Returning to what feels like "home" after being away can make the reentry period challenging for a missionary. Craig Storti writes, "Home is the place where you were born and raised . . . your homeland . . . it refers to a set of feelings and routines as much as to a particular place— where you are known, trusted, accepted, understood, and indulged."[174] Navigating "home" is certainly tied into the ways in which relationally, spiritually, and even financially a church invests in its returning sent ones. As the church provides care in these areas, the missionary will feel a sense of belonging as they return from the field.

Storti further describes this sense of home as being surrounded with familiar places, people, and routines. Missionaries often depart these places, people, and routines and expect them to stay the same, only to come back to a place that looks foreign, relationships that feel distant and awkward, and routines that are disjointed.[175] Missionaries face these and various other challenges as they return from the field, including physical, professional, financial, cultural, social, and educational difficulties.[176] These reentry factors met by reentry behaviors move them from alienation to isolation, reversion to condemnation, and then, finally, to integration.[177] Much like they sought to assimilate when they were acclimating to a new international context, missionaries desire to integrate back into their "home" context with stability. Many factors, though, contribute to an unstable integration, including unexpected circumstances, the speed at which the "newness" hits them, and the close bond they felt with the context and relationships they left behind.[178] As missionaries and sending churches prepare for this reentry period, they should work together to create a plan, and churches should make the effort to be present and to provide pathways for reengaging their sent ones.

---

173 Pollock, Van Reken, and Pollock define "reverse culture shock" as "experiencing culture shock when returning to the passport country rather than a foreign land," 278.

174 Craig Storti, *The Art of Coming Home* (Boston, MA: Intercultural Press, 2003), 3.

175 Ibid., 5–12.

176 Pirolo, *Serving as Senders Today*, 143. Thomas Kimber, "Healthy Reentry: The Shared Responsibility of Missionary Care," *Evangelical Missiological Quarterly* 48, no. 3 (2012), 333–34.

177 Pirolo, *The Reentry Team*, 48.

178 Storti, 28–32.

Planning

Planning on both the missionary's and the sending church's part will require anticipation and intentionality. Thomas Kimber encourages churches to "be aware of reentry challenges, recognize the importance of immediacy (being present from the start of reentry), communicate often with the missionary, and listen well."[179] Churches should assure their missionaries by being a safe place for openness, honesty, and transparency. Planning also involves acknowledging that no one-size-fits-all approach to reentry care exists and that providing appropriate care will require considering variables such as a missionary's length of time on the field, unique needs, and attitudes.[180] Our church put together a process by which we knew six months to a year ahead of time when the missionary would be returning stateside. Because we had a mission house at our disposal, we were able to plan for meeting tangible needs through the house and the amenities it included, as well as helping with schooling and transportation needs. By staying in touch with our missionaries, we were able to get a pulse for what areas we needed to debrief with them on well in advance. Missionaries will not return from the field as the same people they were when they left, and their churches will not be the same either. Zach Bradley notes of missionaries, "They arrive back at churches that have changed, some for the better and some for the worse. They can silently feel quite old, irrelevant, and . . . underutilized."[181] Churches need to be aware of these changes and prepare to work through them as they engage with missionaries during reentry.

Presence

Acts 14:26–28 shows us how important presence is to post-field missionary care. Just as Paul and Barnabas spent "no little time" with the church at Antioch, missionaries need to have significant opportunities to interface with their sending church. This time of interaction as missionaries share stories, successes, difficulties, and challenges is known as debriefing. O'Donnell states, "Missionaries returning from the field need a supportive fellowship where they can debrief, report, rest, and give and receive encouragement."[182]

He further highlights three key areas of reentry support as reflected in Acts 14:

179 Thomas Kimber, "Healthy Reentry: The Shared Responsibility of Missionary Care," *Evangelical Missiological Quarterly* 48, no. 3 (2012), 337–38.

180 Pirolo, *The Reentry Team*, 34–39. On p. 30, Pirolo also accounts for challenges a missionary could face upon reentry if they were not meaningfully involved with the church prior to leaving. He goes on to stress the value of having missionaries serve in leadership capacities for building strong relationships with that church.

181 Bradley, McCrary, Calfee, and Jansen, ch. 2, "Reentry Culture Shock."

182 O'Donnell, *Missionary Care*, 303.

Missionaries should receive a warm and supportive reception, affirming their identity as loved members of the local body and their role and work as missionaries. They should be given adequate time to fully report their mission experience . . . [and] have sufficient opportunity to spend time renewing relationships and experiencing extended fellowship.[183]

Debriefing allows the missionary to share burdens of missionary life with others who will provide a listening ear. Shirley Ralston comments that "without debriefing, life and ministry experiences on the field accumulate, becoming a burden that can affect their health and contribute to burnout."[184] As missionaries from our church returned stateside, one of the associate pastors and I would meet one-on-one with the missionary to debrief in areas of physical, emotional, mental, relational, and spiritual health. We would also provide times for the missionary to meet with our other elders to talk and debrief. Providing these opportunities for the missionary to debrief and share helps the church practice the "one another" commands of Scripture and be a co-laborer like Epaphroditus was for Paul in Philippians 2.

While debriefing can be done from many angles, providing soul care is of the utmost priority. Bradley exhorts the church to "Resist relying on anyone else to provide the rich care that can come from the covenant church community. Fruit will flow from the returning sent one only to the extent that they are refreshed in Christ."[185] Practically, soul care could take the forms of sitting under regular expository preaching, participating in Bible studies, or taking extended times of spiritual retreat. Additionally, there needs to be a time of debrief between the sending church and their missionaries to evaluate the strengths and weaknesses of the on-field care they are receiving (this would include care they receive from their agency and from the church leadership and advocacy teams).[186] Bradley writes, "Ask them questions and lean forward to listen to their answers . . . give them opportunities to share with the church, since all believers are meant to participate in that mission."[187] Debrief can be a vulnerable and often difficult process for missionaries and churches, but it can also expose the church to the best ways to pray, equip, send, and support their missionaries.

183 Ibid., 303.
184 Shirley Ralston, "Healthy at Home: Healthy Minds, Part One: Debriefing," Upstream Collective, 15 June 2021, https://www.upstreamcollective.org/post/healthy-at-home-healthy-minds-part-1-debriefing.
185 Bradley, McCrary, Calfee, and Jansen, ch. 8, "A Critical Ministry."
186 Ibid., ch. 5, "Interview with a Returning Sent One."
187 Ibid.

As churches and partners plan for post-field care and make themselves present for debriefing, the third area in which the church can assist with reintegration is providing on-ramps into the church. Church leaders will need to establish clear avenues and boundaries for ministry as they incorporate their missionaries back into the life of the church. As Bradley writes, "It's easy for them to be either overwhelmed with too much responsibility or under-utilized with too little opportunity."[188] A faithful shepherding church will strike a healthy balance between the two. Avenues for reengaging in ministry ought to provide opportunities to strengthen pre-existing relationships and begin new relationships. Through times of sharing corporately and in small groups, missionaries can speak into the life of the congregation and stoke the missions flame. Thomas Hale and Gene Daniels exhort, "No one better than the missionary can bring the missionary vision to the home church . . . [or] inspire young people to a life of sacrifice and dedication to Jesus."[189] The church must not miss the opportunity to hear from those who serve as an extension of the membership in a cross-cultural context.

188 Ibid., ch. 7, "Welcoming Sent Ones."
189 Hale and Daniels, 487.

A Charge to Churches to Care Well

William Carey certainly charted new waters as he went down into that mine to see India reached with the gospel. Leaving behind comforts and recognizing he'd likely not return "home," he remained committed to the call God had placed on his life, even during the first seven years he labored before seeing a convert. I am sure there were days he wished he could be pulled up by the rope that others were holding for him. Yet, because he remained faithful to his calling, many came to Christ, the Bible was translated into multiple languages, and the church was established in new places. He was able to persevere in the work because he knew he had a band of brothers who were faithfully holding the rope for him on the home front.

The New Testament identifies the local church as that band of brothers and the primary vehicle for sending individuals to proclaim the gospel and establish churches, but many churches have taken a secondary seat in sending, supporting, and receiving their missionaries. Whether it's because they lack time, resources, or knowledge of best practices, they're trying to give deference to the agency, or some combination thereof, churches tend to lean heavily on the sending agency to provide proper care for sent ones. Missionaries who feel the weight of relationship to their sending church along with responsibility to their sending agency often become confused about where their first point of contact in care is. These factors lead to gaps in care, which can cause the missionary to feel isolated, irritated, and ignored by those who should be most invested in them.

While serving for thirteen years as missions pastor in a local church, I worked with missionaries who felt the immense pressures that come with life on the mission field. Whether they were transitioning in their area of service and feeling ill-equipped for their new role, or watching their children struggle to acclimate to life on the field, obeying God's call on their lives brought significant stress and challenges. If no one took on the task of caring well for them, it had the potential to leave them floundering in stress and shift their focus away from ministry. Churches have the opportunity—and the responsibility—to come alongside their sent ones and offer the love and support they need to persevere by caring for them at every stage in their assignment. Missionary care can feel daunting, but it's part of what God calls his church to as we fulfill the "one anothers" of the Christian life, and I pray this book serves as a guide for you and your church as you take the next step in developing your own missionary care strategy. Whether you have yet to send your first missionary or you have already sent several, God has a part for every member of your church to play in sending and supporting your missionaries.

May you be inspired by Gaius's faithfulness, Epaphroditus's sacrifice, and Paul and Barnabas's accountability to their sending church as you create a plan for providing pre-field, on-field, and post-field care to your sent ones. Allow the testimonies of those on the field to reveal the longing your sent ones have for meaningful care and the role it plays in sustaining them as they fulfill their calling. And in turn, understand how the local church can and must provide this kind of care by assessing, equipping, sending, supporting, and receiving their own before, during, and after service on the field. Consider the role that partnership with the mission agency can play in strengthening the support you provide, and allow both church and agency to carry out their roles in missionary care using the resources the Lord has equipped each of them with. Learn from the model churches I've highlighted and the impact that investing in missionary care has played in building strong mission partnerships between sender and sent one. Utilize the resources I've included at the end of this book, or others you may find along the way, as tools to frame your own missionary care strategy.

Finally, determine as a church what the right next steps are for developing a strategy to provide pre-field, on-field, or post-field missionary care. Seek out members who have strong relationships with sent ones and a passion to lead in this ministry, then watch the church labor side by side in caring for your missionaries. Care so much for those you send and support that you can join with Paul in saying, "we were delighted to share with you not only the gospel of God but our lives as well" (1 Thess 2:8). Your sent ones have been called by God to go out from your church to share Christ in another part of the world, and you can help them persevere in declaring, demonstrating, and displaying his gospel as you hold the rope and never let go.

MISSIONARY CARE STRATEGY PROPOSAL

Although churches are often eager to give meaningful care to their missionaries, many churches do not know where to begin. Below is a sample strategy I've outlined that churches can adapt to their context to help them provide adequate pre-field, on-field, and post-field missionary care. With the exception of the final document ("Receiving Returned Missionaries Well"), each of these resources can be accessed by visiting *https://www.theupstreamcollective.org/holdingtherope*.

The Components of the Strategy

While a more exhaustive care strategy could be undertaken, the resources I've listed below will help you take the necessary steps toward providing healthy missionary care. I have grouped these resources as pre-field, on-field, and post-field care components and included the location (either online or in Appendix B) for each. The strategy can be adapted to fit churches of varying contexts, sizes, and approaches to mission.

Pre-Field Care Components

"Sent Ones Self-Assessment and Interview Guide"
The Upstream Collective

An often-overlooked area of missionary care is the pre-field stage. I highlighted in chapter 9 that a thorough assessment is crucial in helping a church determine their sent one's calling, fit, and readiness for the mission field. I have incorporated a self-assessment and interview guide, which helps churches evaluate areas of spiritual, emotional, relational, ministry, and personal health. A missionary needs to have a vibrant, growing relationship with God. They also need to be aware of their emotions and how their past behavior will impact future decisions. They should be able to develop healthy relationships with others as they prepare to join a team on the field. They ought to have a track record of faithful ministry within the context of the local church. Finally, they need to prioritize their personal health. The self-assessment guide helps measure each of these variables and gives the missionary candidate and sending church the opportunity to determine areas that need to be further assessed, addressed, or worked on prior to commissioning.

"Writing a Personal Development Plan"
The Upstream Collective

The second component of pre-field care is a personal development plan. Based on the findings of the self-assessment, this personal development plan helps churches and sent ones answer three questions: What is important for the candidate to know? What kind of person do we want the candidate to be? and What is the most important thing the candidate should be able to do? These questions address practical areas in which the missionary candidate can grow theologically, relationally, and practically.

"Sending Commitment"
The Upstream Collective

The third component of pre-field care is a sending commitment. Missionary care is a two-way street, and missionaries, churches, and agencies ought to covenant together to hold their part of the rope. The covenant outlines areas of commitment in communication, logistics, spirituality, and financial support for the missionary, church, and agency (by way of the field team leader). This type of accountability keeps expectations clear and upheld in missionary care and will aid churches in building long-lasting partnerships.

On-Field Care Components

"Establishing Advocacy Teams"
The Upstream Collective

Chapter 9 underscored the impact of utilizing advocacy teams. These teams of four to eight individuals can provide the link between the church and the mission field by helping care for the missionaries and champion their cause on the field, and by championing the cause of the sending church to the missionaries. Advocacy teams can assist in areas of prayer, communication, logistical coordination, on-field visits, and reentry care. The above resource outlines the importance of advocacy teams, their makeup, their role, and how they function. (For examples of how two churches utilize advocacy teams, see Antioch Church's "Advocate Role Description" and Grand Avenue Baptist Church's "Mission Partnership Advocacy" in Appendix B.).

"Missionary Health Diagnostic" and "Sent One Health Diagnostic"
The Upstream Collective

Just as churches should help their missionaries address different areas of health during the pre-field stage, they should also help them engage in ongoing assessment of those same areas on the field. To that end, I included missionary health diagnostic tools that the missionary and church can utilize in their regular correspondence to assess the following areas: emotional and physical health, marriage and parenting, spiritual formation, ministry engagement, cultural bonding, team and community, relationship with sending organization, and quality of care from the sending church. This tool is meant to aid in the ongoing dialogue and shepherding care that a church should provide for its sent ones.

"Personal Questions Sent Ones Should Ask Regularly"
The Upstream Collective

The fourth on-field component I included is a personal questionnaire that the missionary can use for self-evaluation. This resource asks questions regarding personal health, ministry reflection, emotional health, calling, relationships, and looking forward. These questions are meant to stimulate introspection and personal growth in both the inner and outer life of the missionary.

"Providing Missionary Care When Your Sent Ones Experience a Crisis"
The Upstream Collective

The final on-field care component will help churches care for missionaries in crisis. Churches who are faithfully sending can expect to have missionaries who face crises, and when that happens, the church needs to know how to react. This tool gives practical knowledge on how to respond and who should lead the response.

Post-Field Care Components

Reentry can be an uneasy time for missionaries and churches alike. What once was familiar to the missionary is now foreign, and areas of bonding now seem like barricades to hurdle in conversation. It can be challenging for the missionary to reenter their "home culture" and for the church to know how to receive their sent one and reengage them in the life of the congregation. All these variables, in addition to the logistics of moving back, can create major stress; however, with careful planning, churches can receive their missionaries back in a helpful and meaningful way.

"Crafting an Ideal Furlough"
The Upstream Collective

The first post-field care component is a tool to help churches and missionaries craft an ideal furlough. Stateside assignments should be times of rest, renewal, raising of funds, recruitment, reporting, and refreshment. This tool empowers the church to help their missionaries have a successful return as they seek to accomplish all these goals while balancing time and relationships.

"Preparing for Returning Sent Ones Checklist"
The Upstream Collective

The second post-field care component is a checklist to help missionaries practically think through each area of reentry. This resource will help the church dialogue with their missionary about planning for reentry by establishing expectations, maintaining accountability, and reporting to the church; presence to meet practical needs like airport pickup, debriefing opportunities, and the re-acclimation of children; and provision to meet other physical needs. This checklist ensures no area is overlooked in the reentry process. Walking through particular logistics will help give missionaries confidence as they re-enter their home culture and sending church.

"Returning Sent Ones and Financial Support"
The Upstream Collective

The third post-field care tool is related to financial support. Churches and their missionaries should both be clear on expectations about support once missionaries have returned. This resource helps churches think through providing ongoing support and helps their sent ones think through possible financial variables.

"Receiving Returned Missionaries Well"
The Summit Church
Appendix B

The fourth and final post-field care component is more comprehensive re-entry process. I adapted this from a resource utilized by The Summit Church in Raleigh-Durham, North Carolina. This process utilizes advocacy teams and assigns team members and other church members with responsibilities to assist in the reentry phase. While this process is geared toward larger churches, smaller churches will be able to incorporate certain elements as they develop their reentry process.

APPENDIX B

Missionary Care Strategy Examples

Each of these resources has been included here with the written permission of the churches that created them.

Pre-Field, On-Field, and Post-Field Components

"Sending Covenant," Antioch Church, Louisvlle, Kentucky

"Advocacy Teams," Antioch Church, Louisville, Kentucky

"Mission Partnership Advocacy," Grand Avenue Baptist Church, Fort Smith, Arkansas

"Receiving Returned Missionaries Well," The Summit Church, Raleigh-Durham, North Carolina

Missionary Care Strategies

"Missionary Care Process," Cornerstone Church, Ames, Iowa

"Missionary Care Overview," Sojourn East, Louisville, Kentucky

"Missionary Care Strategy," The Summit Church, Raleigh-Durham, North Carolina

"Sender and Sent One Expectations," Reliant Mission Agency, Orlando, Florida

ANTIOCH
CHURCH

Sending Covenant

The Scriptures provide rich examples of the relationships God desires between sending churches and sent ones (Acts 13-14, Philippians, 3 John 6-8). Antioch thus seeks to follow those examples through a Sending Covenant. This covenant helps both Antioch and distributed members understand their responsibilities in these sacred relationships.

Antioch commits to:

1. Praying for distributed members and the people they serve in Sunday Gatherings, Family Groups, Missionary Care Team, and our households.
2. Overseeing and cultivating the effectiveness of Advocates.
3. Providing care visits with the goal of one per term. Stateside visits and urgent needs will be taken into consideration as visits are planned.
4. Being available as Pastors and Advocates to provide care and counsel. Advocates will communicate any such requests to the Pastors.
5. Maintaining sensitivity to secure communication.
6. Providing logistical support and opportunities to report during stateside visits.
7. Providing the ongoing financial support agreed upon prior to commissioning.

Distributed members commit to:

1. Recognize and relate to Antioch Pastors as having a significant, ongoing place at the table in your life.
2. Continuing to participate in the life of Antioch through relationships, prayer, and giving of resources.
3. Responding in a timely manner to communication from Advocates, the Deacon of Sending, and Pastors.
4. Sending monthly updates for the sake of ongoing relationship and prayer.
5. Maintaining open and honest communication with Advocates.
6. Spending ⅓ of their stateside visit in Louisville in order to participate at Antioch.

Distributed:_____   Antioch:_____

Antioch Church
Missionary Care Team/Advocates
Roles and Responsibilities

MCT member expectations:

Meet Monthly.
Pray over our missionaries.
Organize "Share Services".
Calendar and other Fund Raising/Awareness Campaigns.
Act as an advocate for the MCT. Point people to information and resources and they have questions or desire to communicate with a missionary family.
Organize prayer requests and updates on each missionary and post to the City within 24hrs of each monthly meeting.

Advocate Responsibilities:

Monthly Meeting - As an advocate you agree to commit to attend monthly MCT meetings.

Stay Connected - Part of providing care to missionaries is staying connected. Your missionary should hear from you at least once per month. This can happen through text, email, Skype, FaceTime, handwritten letters, Facebook Messenger, etc. There are any number of creative ways to communicate. It is up to you to determine which method seems preferable to your missionary. Make it easy for them.

Gather Information - Part of the reason to stay connected to your missionary is purely relational. Our desire is to pursue intentional gospel relationships to display Christ's glory among the nations. Staying in regular communication with our missionaries is one of the most tangible expressions of this pursuit.

Another reason to stay in touch is to become and remain informed about the life of your missionary. This should include a wide range matters including but not limited to physical health, spiritual health, relational health, ministry updates, matters for prayer, travel plans etc.

One more reason it is important to remain in regular communication with your missionary is to share with them what is happening stateside, particularly with Antioch and our ministries. Our desire is to help them remain informed and feel closely connected with what is taking place here.

Share Information - As an advocate you agree to prepare an update to share at each monthly MCT meeting. Your update will be summarized and documented for various distribution purposes.

Connect Others - As an advocate you agree to act as point person for anyone wanting to communicate with one of our missionaries in any way. Ultimately the missionary will have final say in who they communicate with and how. However, upon initial contact, your role is to gather that persons info and send it to your missionary along with their request in the manner your missionary has indicated is their preference. This takes into consideration any security concerns or communication limitations that are unique to the missionary.

Mission Partnership Advocacy (MPA)

Each of our national and international partnerships will have a MPA with a leader over that group.

Each MPA is responsible for:
1. Supporting the missionaries in your partnership - This could include keeping up with the missionaries' birthdays, sending gifts for Christmas, writing letters of encouragement, handling the organization of things to take when a trip happens, etc.
2. Connecting the partnership to our church and Educating our church about the partnership - This could include distributing missionary newsletters, writing posts on the mission blog, including an article in the mission newsletter, setting up a booth at events, keeping your website up to date, talking to people about the partnership, etc.
3. Recruiting more people to the partnership - This could include intentionally recruiting new people for trips, inviting new people to the meetings, talking personally to people about the partnership, signing people up using the web and/or social media, etc.
4. Planning and Organizing Strategic Mission Trips - This will be done with support from the mission pastor and using the software, eFurther.
5. Praying for the partnership - This includes not just praying as a team, but mobilizing prayer church-wide in creative ways.

Each MPA Leader is responsible for:
1. Serving a 3-year term.
2. Organizing a meeting with your MPA group at least 4 times per year.
3. Meeting with the other MPA Leaders and the Mission Pastor twice per year.
4. Organizing your MPA group in such a way that others are doing the different responsibilities outlined above (delegation).
5. Giving overall vision to your MPA group, pushing them to do their tasks and providing an environment for your group to be creative in accomplishing those tasks.

Receiving Returned Missionaries Well

The Summit Church – Raleigh, North Carolina

Receiving by the church (not merely returning by the missionary) is the culmination of sending. The church is responsible for her sent ones from the time they express interest in missions until they have returned and have and been fully reintegrated into the life of their church and re-established sustainable life rhythms. The returning and receiving stage of sending is often the most neglected, because it is the easiest to neglect, part of the process.

Extra care and intentionality have to be put forth in order to help ensure that missionaries leaving the field start a new stage of life stateside in the most healthy way possible.

Although executed in an organic way, the receiving process should be a planned and detailed process. Once a missionary has been away for one or more years and those who know and love them haven't seen them, then what is not planned will likely not occur organically.

The leader of the receiving and returning process is the advocate. The advocate is the person who is primarily responsible for supporting the missionary while they are on the field, and ensuring that other church members are supporting the missionary as well. This makes the advocate the liaison between the missionary and the church while the missionary is on the field, and so the advocate should play a similar role in the missionary's returning process.

In this process, the advocate's main role is to lead the care team (which is compiled of 4-8 people) who are taking primary responsibility for caring for the returned missionary. The care team is the group of people within the church that is acting on behalf of the church to care for the missionary within this process. Every stage of this process will be primarily carried out by the advocate and the care team.

But how? Here is an example of a "process document" that corresponds with every care activity that needs to occur. This is what the advocate uses to communicate with and synchronize the efforts of the care team. *The process document is a master document that should contain updates from everyone involved on how the missionary is doing in key areas.* We suggest using a platform like Google Docs that allows different people to update the document so that everyone can see the changes and no single person is responsible for receiving info, editing a Word doc, and sending the updates back to everyone.

This document (see example to follow) should give you – whether you're a pastor or a lay advocate – a step-by-step process for receiving a returning missionary by (a) helping them debrief their experiences, (b) handle life struggles associated with their transition back to the states, (c) start a new stage of life, and (d) be reintegrated into the life of your church.

There will be certain aspects that need to be added to this or taken out of it based the unique situation of each church, individual, or family, but you can use this process as a grid. If you're a missionary, you can use this document to be proactive in your own returning process by initiating these things and asking your sending church to do these things for you.

The Process

The process of returning begins at least four to six weeks prior to the missionary getting on an airplane headed towards America. The preparation for receiving needs to begin by the care team during this same time period.

30-45 Days from Return Date

Preparing to receive a missionary well is only possible if the advocate has been supporting the missionary well during their time on the field. Monthly communication should be the standard for supporting a missionary.

If monthly communication is happening, and there is an adequate depth to those conversations, the advocate should know when the missionary plans to return home and whether or not that return is permanent. *This is the first step in the returning process: knowing when the missionary plans to return home.*

When the missionary decides to return home, the advocate should begin the receiving and returning process. Action Step One (Advocate Led): Create your own copy of the Google Document send a copy to each care team member (who should already be in place and supporting the missionary), and begin filling in key information for a comprehensive receiving plan.

Action Step Two (Advocate Led): The next action step is to help your missionary friend plan well for their transition on both sides: transitioning out of their role overseas well and transitioning into the next phase of life in America well.

Email your missionary friend about the following tasks. *In the weeks ahead let them know you are praying over these conversations and details.* These can be emotionally weighty tasks marked by a mixture of grief and excitement.

1. Communicate a firm date to you team lead and stateside pastor for when you are returning.
2. That date is:

e. Make a list of team members and national friends and leaders with whom you want to say an intentional goodbye.

4. Make a list of key transitions you anticipate as you engage life in the United States again. These are points that the advocate wants to communicate with the care team in order to begin brainstorming how to best assist with these transitions.]
    i. Residence
    ii. Work
    iii. School for children
    iv. Other
5. Talk with my international team lead to discern how to best delegate my current responsibilities and transition out of my role well.

Action Step Three (Advocate Led): Prepare for the day your missionary friend is returning and their immediate needs that will happen upon their initial arrival.

1. Find the exact date, time, and flight numbers
2. Work with the care team to secure immediate housing and transportation for the missionary.
3. Work with the care team to plan an airport welcome (including as many church members as possible) for the returning missionary.
4. Make a care package for the returning missionary for either the airport welcome or to be left at their residence.
5. Plan a returning celebration party to help church members celebrate what God has done in the missionary life and work. The size and tone of this celebration should be planned with the personality and season of life of the returning missionary in mind.
6. Plan to celebrate their returning during corporate worship. Principle: *You will replicate what you celebrate.* The return of a missionary is a discipleship and spiritual formation opportunity for your entire congregation.

First 30 Days after Returning

Action Step Four (Advocate Coordinated): After the missionary gets settled, the next step for the advocate and care team is to meet with the missionary. The meeting should consist of the advocate, several members of the care team, and at least one pastor. The meeting can be held at the church or not, but the environment should be conducive for honest and private conversation. The main thrust of this initial meeting is to care for them through *hearing their story.* This will primarily be a time of listening and asking questions for the care team.

· For guidance on good questions see: bradhambrick.com/5missiondebriefs

For every meeting the advocate or care team has with the missionary, there should be some set-aside time of prayer. Nothing that the advocate or care team does by itself can fight the spiritual warfare that the missionary will be enduring.

Intentional, Informal Engagement (Document Planned): This is not a "step" per say but is vitally important to receiving a missionary well – each care team member should intentionally seek out face- to-face time with their missionary friend in the month after their return.

A member of the care team should see the missionary in person at least once a week. Every member of the care team should see the missionary at least once in person (outside of corporate worship) during this first month.

The advocate must ensure that every care team member has the mindset of *hearing the story* of the missionary during these times (see: bradhambrick.com/5missiondebriefs).

Each care team member should update the care team about their conversations so that (a) these conversations are not overly redundant, and (b) the missionary has an increasing sense of being known during their first month at home.

Action Step Five (Pastor Planned): During the first month the missionary is stateside the church should host a celebration/reception for members of the church to reconnect with the missionary. This should have been planned before the missionary returns, but can happen within 2-4 weeks of the missionary's return.

The details of this celebration can fit the personality of the missionary and your church, but the main goals are to make the missionary feel loved and celebrated, create an environment where church members and staff can reconnect with the missionary, and emphasize the importance of your sent ones to the church.

Action Step Six (Pastor Planned): Within the first month, the missionary should be welcomed and celebrated from stage during corporate worship on the weekend. This accomplishes three things:

1. Make the missionary feel significantly remembered for what they did.
2. Helps the congregation remember the missionary.

3. Reinforces that you replicate what you celebrate. A church member's journey to joining the mission of God could start with seeing what someone else has done for the mission.

Additional Care Available (Pastor Communicated; Team Aware): Counseling Availability – Prior your missionary friend's return the church's policy regarding the availability and potential scholarship for formal counseling should be communicated. As the care team has deeper conversations with the missionary the need for this counseling resource may emerge.

Possible topics could include: grief related to former role and distance from international friends, conflict emerging from transitions in major life systems and culture, depression, emergence of post traumatic symptoms from significant painful or dangerous events while overseas, a sense that their role in God's mission is less significant now that they're not overseas, etc...

In their mild forms, you may be able to walk with the missionary as they grow out of these struggles (topically arranged Christian counseling resource can be found at: bradhambrick.com). There may come a time when your ability to help them grow in these areas ceases, however.

When you sense that you're getting beyond your ability to help (bradhambrick.com/faq6), you should have a Christian counselor or Christian counseling center that you trust to be able to refer them to.

If you do not know a trusted Christian counselor here is guidance on finding one:

· bradhambrick.com/findacounselor

If possible, you should cover at least some of the cost for counseling out of the church missions budget. A good rule of thumb is to cover the first four sessions of counseling and then meet to evaluate if more sessions are needed.

30-60 Days After Return

Action Step Seven (Advocate Coordinated): Around 60 days after the missionary family has returned, the advocate and care team should have another collective face-to-face meeting. This meeting can be less formal, but should still intentionally cover at least four question clusters (the order of question should be arranged for what best honors the needs of the returned missionary):

First Question Cluster – Spiritual Life: How's your devotional and prayer life been recently? How have you been able to re-engage into the life of our church? Have you returned to your small group or visited a new one? Have you began serving anywhere? Do you see yourself being able to grow and thrive here long-term?

A returned missionary family is an incredible asset to our church, so we should encourage them to begin coaching other future missionaries, supporting current missionaries, or being involved in local outreach.

Second Question Cluster – Life Direction: What's next? Are you considering going back to the mission field in some way? Are you considering going back to school? Have you decided on another career path? Have you taken any steps for any of these options?

Third Question Cluster – Church Assessment: What can we do better? The returned missionary family can give an honest and helpful assessment of how we, as a church, are supporting our missionaries.

You can ask how the training they received did or did not prepare them well, if they felt supported and frequently contacted during their time, and if there was another part of the sending process that was helpful or harmful.

Fourth Question Cluster – Personal Flourishing: How are you doing? (A) Personal Health - Have you been struggling with any negative emotions since having returned? How has your sleep patterns, exercising, eating, etc. been?

(B) Purposeful Progress - Do you feel like you're stuck? Do you feel like you're growing? Do you have a plan to continue to grow in this season?

(C) Journey Evaluation - What have been some hard things about this season? What have been some encouraging things about this season?

· Note: This meeting should create the agenda for the care team moving forward. If a consistent and healthy level of interaction has been occurring between the care team and the returned missionary, then there should be few surprises in this meeting.

Ongoing Informal Care (Document Planned): Every care team member should have a face-to-face meeting with the missionary during this time. The advocate should ensure that the team members are planning these meetings and have intentional questions prepared.

Each care team member should continue to send a weekly email to care team giving a summary of interactions and conversations between care team members and the missionary.

60-90 Days After Return

Action Step Eight (Advocate Coordinated): In the third month after the missionary has returned, the advocate and every member of the care team should have another check-in with the missionary. The nature of this check-in will depend on how the missionary has been doing.

If the missionary has been struggling in several areas, this check-in should be face-to-face and intentional based around their pressing need(s).

If the missionary has been thriving and doing great, either a face-to-face meeting or phone call could work.

The goal of this stage is to make sure the missionary has been reintegrated into the life of your church and is healthy and growing.

Questions to ask at this stage are: How have you been able to re-engage in the life of our church? Have you been able to rebuild significant community around you? Have you taken a next step toward whatever God has for you next in terms of career, education, and residence? Is there anything else our church can do for you?

At this point, if the advocate and church staff think the missionary is healthy and growing, the formal process of receiving the missionary can end. This process can and should be prolonged based on significant issues that the missionary needs more help in continuing to walk through.

Formally ending the receiving process with the care team should include encouraging them to continue to walk with the missionary as friends and fellow church members.

CORNERSTONE
GLOBAL

MISSIONARY CARE PROCESS
GLOBAL DEVELOPMENT WORKSHEET #6

See Missionary Care for More Ideas

Strategic Pre-Field Care
- Assess people well on the front end so they do not create tons of challenges on the field.
- Challenge character issues in their life pre-field. Yellow lights in the US are red lights overseas (See Development Opportunities for PDPs).
- Assess their personality and help them be self-aware so their motivations continue in their purity (Enneagram; Strengths Finder,etc.)
- Work through their PDP's with them.
- Send people to great, healthy teams with IMB or C2C teams that will take care of people.

Proactive On-Field Care
- Send Missionary Care trips with no purpose, but to hang out and provide an enjoyable week for missionaries.
- Advocacy Teams through Connection Groups for each missionary.
- Pray for them on Mondays with staff.
- Check in on how they are doing with team leaders regularly.
- Provide counseling as necessary for people on the field (7051-005 in the budget)
- Regular phone calls. Minimum 2x/year per missionary from the Missions Pastor.

Reactive On-Field Care
- Connect with their team leader on shepherding issues; Connection with Member Care counselors from their sending organization.
- Consider sending a good friend over for refreshment for the missionary.
- Consider getting them out of their area of work and to a beach or to a good conference.

Stateside/Furlough Care
- Lunch and Learns - Provide opportunities for them to share their story with leadership, small groups, mid-sized groups, and potentially the church.
- Get them some time with a counselor that will ask them good questions and help them process an issues (don't under-estimate the power of this one)
- Ask them some good questions. Re-Entry Questions for Stateside/Furlough
- Provide one of the Global vehicles for them.

Returner Care
- Read: *Returning Well* by Melissa Chaplin
- Read: *Burn Up or Splash Down* by Marion Knell
- Go through some re-entry sessions with returners (See "Questions for Returners")
- Have them work with a counselor or send them to a re-entry organization.

Good Missionary Care Resources
- *Mind the Gaps: Engaging the Church in Missionary Care* by David J. Wilson
- *Burn Up or Splash Down* by Marion Knell
- *Returning Well* by Michelle Chaplin
- *First Thirty Daze* by Larry & Susan McCrary

Care for Parents of Missionaries
- Monthly Zoom Meeting
- Blog
- Videos

Times for Missionary Care
- Around holidays and birthdays
- Around the 6 month mark of going overseas when the honeymoon period is over.

Sojourn East Missionary Care Overview

Sending Staff - Big picture support

Responsibilities: Overall leadership of care volunteers

- Emergency and crisis care coordination
- Sending agency member care collaboration
- Field visits
- Stateside debriefing

Care Team - Ongoing encouragement

Responsibilities:

- Monthly conversations with sent ones for encouragement and accountability
- Prayer
- Missionary care training participation

Volunteer characteristics: Care-minded, spiritually mature, heart for the nations and/or global workers, healthy marriage, exceptional listener, overseas experience (desired, not required)

Crisis Team - Emergency professional support

Responsibilities:

- Intervention and counseling for crises such as grief, trauma, debilitating sin issues, emotional/psychological breakdown, conflict, and severe medical problems
- Field visits, when necessary

Volunteer characteristics: Counseling, mental-health, and medical professionals; East elders and staff pastors; Sending staff

Kid Team - MK encouragement

Responsibilities:

- Birthday gifts and "thinking of you" notes/cards
- SojournKids missionary prayer
- Stateside debriefing

Volunteer characteristics: Knowledgeable of TCK (Third Culture Kid) needs, administratively gifted

Home Team - Stateside practical help

Responsibilities:

- Stateside housing, transportation, and other needs coordination
- Planning for sharing and prayer events
- Development of resource list for stateside missionaries

Volunteer characteristics: Administratively gifted, well-connected within church body, heart for practical service

Summit Missionary Care

The Church Working Together to Care Well for Our Missionaries

Summit Missionary Care is the intentional partnership between Summit Advocates, the Summit missions staff, Summit campuses, and Summit small groups to provide member care for missionaries (either individuals or families) sent from The Summit Church to the nations. The roles of each partner in the Summit Missionary Care Program are below.

A Summit Advocate

An Advocate is a Summit member who participates in the mission of God by being the primary conduit to connect the church (small groups, campus staff, and missions staff) to a specific missionary and the missionary to the church. They are asked to maintain a rhythm of at least one voice-to-voice conversation with their missionary per month for the purpose of accountability and prayer. Advocates submit a monthly report to the Summit missions team in order to ensure adequate support.

The Summit Missions Staff

Each member of the Summit missions staff commits to maintaining regular contact with missionaries in order to provide support and accountability. Missions staff members participate in quarterly conference calls with missionaries and hold advocates accountable by reviewing monthly reports. They also assist in coordinating support for missionaries on stateside visits, particularly through maintaining missionary housing and vehicles.

A Summit Campus

The home campus of each missionary is tasked with providing encouragement and support via their campus staff. They coordinate commissioning services and receive and respond to missionary updates. They plan "welcome back" stage times and assist in supporting missionaries on stateside visits. They also aid in recruiting for short-term trips to visit their missionaries.

Summit Small Groups

Each Summit small group is challenged to commit to supporting one missionary. They accomplish this by reading regular updates from their missionary, praying for requests missionaries share, and responding to updates with encouragement. Small groups also send care packages as needed (at least one time a year) and participate in short-term trips to visit their missionary.

One Additional Support: Summit Encourager Network Team (SENT)

SENT, comprised of lay members at the Summit, complements existing Summit staff efforts in missionary care and increases the amount and type of intentional care that is given to field workers. SENT members serve as coaches and mentors as missionaries prepare for overseas work. They dedicate regular times for intercessory prayer for those on the field. They often serve as "first responders" to visit and bring encouragement and care to missionaries in crisis. Finally, they seek to help missionaries at the end of their mission work adjust to life back in the states.

RELIANT

Sending Church | Goer Expectations

We are excited that you have a member of your church that is considering or has already chosen to work with Reliant as their sending agency. We believe that the Bible gives churches an important role in sending missionaries. Specifically those who have been called to cross cultures to bring the Gospel in Word and in Deed.

It is important as your Sent One goes out to define the role between the Sending Church and the Sent One. Defining these roles will help both parties to be first of all drawn to a vision. But secondly to avoid let down. Clear is kind. While this relationship will never be perfect, being clear from the beginning of what the sending church relationship with the Goer and vice versa should look like will greatly mitigate the risk of relational fallout.

In this document we have endeavored to outline some various levels of relationship between the sending church and the Goer. Here's how this table works:

1. Below, on the first column, are categories of what a sending church can do.
2. Each of the following 3 columns gives varying levels of commitment that the sending church could potentially fulfill.
3. Sending churches: For each category, bold the level of responsibility you would like to take on for each category. You may bold if you prefer to be called a supporting church over a sending church, be clear with your Goer about that.

*As a note, you can also think about these levels as tiers of the type of sending church you will be for various Goers from your church. Maybe some of your best are in the Tier 1 (Advanced) category. Maybe your middle of the road Goers are Tier 2 (Intermediate). Maybe your Tier 3 (Entry) category are for those you have little connection with, but want to bless.

Categories	Entry Level Sending Church (Tier 3)	Intermediate Level Sending Church (Tier 2)	Advanced Level Sending Church (Tier 1)
Missions Staffing	Volunteer Missions Point Person	Staff Member with Missions in their job description	Full-time Missions staff
Communication with the Goer	Video call with Goer at minimum every 6 months.	Video call with Goer at minimum every 3 months.	Video call with Goer at minimum every
Member Care Contact	Church Member	Elder or staff member	Elder or staff member.
Prayer	Volunteer is praying for the Goer	A small group is praying for the Goer.	There is an opportunity during a Sunday morning to pray for the Goer.

Assessment of Potential Goer	Fill out a reference during Reliant application process.	Implement a basic church assessment form for the Goer. Commission them publicly.	Implement a church assessment & development process for the Goer.
Commissioning	Share in the church newsletter that they are Going.	Provide a space for a small gathering of people to send them.	Commission them on a Sunday morning.
Field Supervisory Role	Entrust supervision to the field leadership	Entrust supervision to the field leadership. Get regular times of interaction with field leader.	Entrust supervision to the field leadership. Find someone on your church to be on the board of the Goers organization, or to regularly interact with the team leader to stay up to speed on the impact of the ministry.
Short-term trips	No organized short-term trips	Sending regular short-term trips to Goer yearly or more. Send someone important in their lives to visit them every 2-3 years.	Send regular short-term trips to Goer, as well as elder/staff vision trips. Send someone important in their lives once a year.
Relationship to Goer's Field Supervisor	Yearly video calls or emails around evaluations.	Build relationship with supervisor in order to know how Goers are really doing.	Regular relationship building with supervisor.
Funding	Give 0-5% of Goer's budget	Give 5-10% of Goer's budget	Give 10-20% of Goer's budget.
Goer Evaluations with Agency	Reading evaluations are optional.	Read evaluations from missions agency for Goer.	Conduct evaluations with Goers, or do alongside their supervisor.
Updates	Read updates. Respond periodically	Read updates and respond.	Get members of your church to signup to a Goers updates.
Furlough Church Reporting	Allow them the chance to meet with a small group(s) when hos.	Lunch & Learn opportunity available for Goer to share and members to voluntarily attend.	Sunday morning On-stage report. Staff/elder meeting report
Furlough Care	Staff member meets with them on furlough	Counseling sessions for debrief paid for by the church.	Send to debriefing conference or retreat with a group that specializes in it.
Provisions for Furlough	Church small group to attend	Connection to a small group. Potentially	Small group, Housing, and Vehicle.

		providing housing or a vehicle.	
Long-term Sending	No promise of sending long term to the Goer's team	Work towards sending long-term members to the Goer	Feel a weight of responsibility to send to the team

Role of the Goer

- Treat the sending church with generosity. Remember "out of sight, out of mind" is a hard thing to overcome.
- Share needs with your sending church rather than expecting them to know your needs.
- Send out regular updates (every 1-2 months) of varying length and to varying group sizes. Always simple and with pictures.
- Give plenty of notice prior to a furlough. At least 6 months.
- Receive short-term trips well.
- Provide long term pathways to your city for interested sending church members.

In order to be considered a sending church for a Reliant Goer, we would ask you to consider, at minimum becoming an Entry-Level Sending Church with that Goer. If this is not possible, we'd encourage you to communicate to that Goer that you would like to be a supporting church for them, but not a sending church.

Want more information? The Reliant International Team is equipped and passionate about walking sending churches through how they can grow in caring for missionaries. Please reach out to international@reliant.org if you would like to converse around this topic.

BIBLIOGRAPHY

Akin, Daniel L. *1, 2, 3 John*. New American Commentary 38. Nashville, TN: Holman Reference, 2001.

Akin, Daniel L., Benjamin L. Merkle, and George G. Robinson. *40 Questions About the Great Commission*. Edited by Benjamin L. Merkle. Grand Rapids, MI: Kregel, 2020.

Allen, Roland. *Missionary Methods: St. Paul's or Ours? A Study of the Church in the Four Provinces*. Rev. ed. Monee, IL: Pantianos Classics, 2018.

Ashford, Bruce R., ed. *Theology and Practice of Mission: God, the Church, and the Nations*. Nashville, TN: B&H Academic, 2011.

Baptist Missionary Society. *Periodical Accounts Relative to a Society Formed Among the Particular Baptist for Propagating the Gospel Among the Heathen*. London, UK: J.W. Morris, 1800, no. 1 p. 3. http://www.wmcarey.edu/carey/per-acct-vol1/bms-founding.pdf.

Barker, Glenn W. "1, 2, and 3 John." The Expositor's Bible Commentary 12. Edited by Frank E. Gaebelein. Grand Rapids, MI: Zondervan, 1981.

Beirn, Steve and George W. Murray. Well Sent: *Reimagining the Church's Missionary-Sending Process*. Fort Washington, PA: CLC, 2015.

Bell, Bradley. *The Sending Church Defined*. 2nd ed. Knoxville, TN: The Upstream Collective, 2020.

Bock, Darrell L. *A Theology of Luke and Acts: Biblical Theology of the New Testament*. Grand Rapids, MI: Zondervan, 2012.

———. *Acts*. Baker Exegetical Commentary on the New Testament. Grand Rapids, MI: Baker Academic, 2007.

Bradley, Zach. "A Practical Way to Structure Your Church's Missionary Care." International Mission Board. 31 May 2017. https://www.imb.org/2017/05/31/practical-way-structure-church-missionary-care/.

Bradley, Zach, Susan McCrary, Rodney Calfee, and Andy Jansen. *Receiving Sent Ones During Reentry: The Challenges of Coming "Home" and How Churches Can Help*. The Upstream Collective: CreateSpace, 2017.

Burns, E.D. *The Missionary Theologian: Sent into the World, Sanctified by the Word*. Ross-shire, Great Britain: Christian Focus, 2020.

Bushong, Lois. *Belonging Everywhere and Nowhere: Insights into Counseling the Globally Mobile.* Indianapolis, IN: Mango Tree Intercultural Services, 2013.

Carey, S. Pearce. *Samuel Pearce, M.A., The Baptist Brainerd.* London, UK: The Carey Press, 1934.

———. *William Carey.* London, UK: Hodder & Stoughton, 1923.

Cook III, William F. and Chuck Lawless. *Spiritual Warfare in the Storyline of Scripture.* Nashville, TN: B&H Academic, 2019.

Crider, Caleb, Larry McCrary, Rodney Calfee, and Wade Stephens. *Tradecraft: For the Church on Mission.* Portland, OR: Urban Loft, 2013.

Crossman, Tanya. *Misunderstood: The Impact of Growing Up Overseas in the 21st Century.* United Kingdom: Summertime Publishing, 2016.

Daub, Anna. "How the Local Church Can Support Single Women on the Mission Field." Upstream Collective. 9 March 2020. https://www.theupstreamcollective.org/post/how-the-local-church-can-support-single-women-on-the-mission-field/.

DeYoung, Kevin and Greg Gilbert. *What Is the Mission of the Church?* Wheaton, IL: Crossway, 2011.

Fee, Gordon D. *Paul's Letter to the Philippians.* New International Commentary on the New Testament. Grand Rapids, MI: Eerdmans, 1995.

Finn, Nathan A. and Keith S. Whitfield, eds. *Spirituality for the Sent: Creating a New Vision for the Missional Church.* Downers Grove, IL: InterVarsity Press, 2017.

Ford, Deborah. "P(r)ay as they Go? Re-examining the Role of the Local Church in Cross-cultural Missionary Care." *Evangel* 22.1 (2004): 4–10.

Fowl, Stephen E. *Philippians.* The Two Horizons New Testament Commentary. Grand Rapids, MI: Eerdmans, 2005.

Fuller, Andrew. *A Heart for Missions: A Classic Memoir of Samuel Pearce.* Birmingham, AL: Solid Ground Christian Books, 2006.

Garland, David E. "Ephesians–Philemon." The Expositor's Bible Commentary 12. Rev. ed. Edited by Tremper Longman III and David E. Garland. Grand Rapids, MI: Zondervan, 2006.

George, Timothy. *Faithful Witness: The Life and Mission of William Carey.* Birmingham, AL: New Hope, 1991.

Greear, J. D. *Gaining by Losing: Why the Future Belongs to Churches That Send.* Grand Rapids, MI: Zondervan, 2015.

Haguewood, Jamie. "Missionaries Abroad Need Friendships Back Home," Reaching & Teaching Blog. 8 December 2020. https://rtim.org/missionaries-abroad-need-friendships-back-home/.

Hale, Thomas and Gene Daniels. *On Being a Missionary.* Rev. ed. Littleton, CO: William Carey Library, 2012.

Hansen, G. Walter. *The Letter to the Philippians.* Pillar New Testament Commentary. Grand Rapids, MI: Eerdmans, 2009.

Harrison, Jeanne. *Hiding in the Hallway: Anchoring Yourself as an MK.* Birmingham, AL: New Hope, 2017.

Hawthorne, Gerald F. and Ralph P. Martin. *Philippians.* World Bible Commentary 43. Rev. ed. Edited by Bruce M. Metzger, David A. Hubbard, and Glenn W. Barker. Grand Rapids, MI: Zondervan, 2004.

Hay, Rob. *Worth Keeping: Global Perspectives on Best Practice in Missionary Retention.* Pasadena, CA: William Carey Library, 2007.

Haykin, Michael A.G. *The Missionary Fellowship of William Carey.* Sanford, FL: Reformation Trust, 2018.

Hellerman, Joseph H. *Exegetical Guide to the Greek New Testament: Philippians.* Edited by Andreas J. Kösteberger and Robert W. Yarbrough. Nashville, TN: B&H Academic, 2015.

Hibbert, Evelyn and Richard Hibbert. *Training Missionaries: Principles and Possibilities.* Pasadena, CA: William Carey Library, 2016.

International Bulletin of Missionary Research. Vol. 39, No. 1. Retrieved from http://www.internationalbulletin.org/issues/2015-01/2015-01-ibmr-lo-res.pdf.

"International Mission Board: About Us." International Mission Board. https://www.imb.org/about.

Ironside, Mike. "Four Types of Sending Churches: Missionary Care Sending Church." Upstream Collective. 7 May 2021. http://www.theupstreamcollective.org/ post/four-types-of-sending-churches-missionary-care-sending-church.

————. "The Sending Pipeline: From U.S. Senders or Potential Goers to Committed Goers." Upstream Collective. 27 September 2021. https://www.theupstreamcollective.org/post/the-sending-pipeline-from-us-senders-or-potential-goers-to-committed-goers.

Jennings, Steve. "What Would Happen If You Sent Your Best?" *9 Marks Journal: Missions* (Fall 2015): 41–42.

Joannes, David. The Mind of a Missionary: *What Global Kingdom Workers Tell Us About Thriving on Mission Today.* Prescott, AZ: Within Reach Global, 2018.

Johnson, Andy. *Missions: How the Local Church Goes Global.* Wheaton, IL: Crossway, 2017.

Keener, Craig S. *Acts: An Exegetical Commentary: 3:1–14:28.* Vol. 2. Grand Rapids, MI: Baker Academic, 2013.

Kimber, Thomas. "Healthy Reentry: The Shared Responsibility of Missionary Care." *Evangelical Missiological Quarterly* 48, no. 3 (2012): 332–38.

Krentz, Edgar. "Civic Culture and the Philippians." *Currents in Theology and Mission* 35, no. 4 (August 2008): 258–63.

Kruse, Colin G. *The Letters of John.* Pillar New Testament Commentary. Grand Rapids, MI: Eerdmans, 2000.

Lane, Timothy S. and Paul David Tripp. *How People Change.* 2nd ed. Greensboro, NC: New Growth, 2008.

Marshall, I. Howard, *The Epistles of John.* The New International Commentary on the New Testament. Grand Rapids, MI: Eerdmans, 1978.

Marshman, John Clark. *The Life and Times of Carey, Marshman, and Ward.* William Carey University, https://www.wmcarey.edu/carey/jcmarshman/lifetimes.htm.

Martin, Ralph. *Philippians.* Tyndale New Testament Commentary 11. 3rd ed. Downers Grove, IL: InterVarsity Press, 1959, 1987, 2008.

McCrary, Susan. "How the Church Can Care for Their Third-Culture Kids." Ethics and Religious Liberty Commission. 8 February 2021. https://erlc.com/resource-library/articles/how-the-church-can-care-for-their-third-culture-kids/.

Melick, Jr., Richard R. *Philippians, Colossians, Philemon*. New American Commentary 32. Nashville, TN: Holman Reference, 1991.

Menikoff, Aaron. *Character Matters: Shepherding in the Fruit of the Spirit*. Chicago, IL: Moody, 2020.

———. "Don't Just Be a Sending Church, Be a Staying Church," Reaching & Teaching Blog. 24 November 2020, https://rtim.org/dont-just-be-a-sending-church-be-a-staying-church/.

Miller, Joe, Ben Marshall and Sandra Murray. "Church-Driven Soul Care for Overseas Missionaries." Biblical Counseling Coalition. 24 March 2021. www.biblical counselingcoalition.org/2021/03/24/the-local-church-as-an-equipping-and-long-term-care-instrument-for-sending-overseas-missionaries/.

Morden, Peter. *Offering Christ to the World: Andrew Fuller (1754–1815) and the Revival of Eighteenth Baptist Century Particular Baptist Life*. Studies in Baptist History and Thought 8. Carlisle: Paternoster, 2003.

Murray, Taylor. *Hidden in My Heart: A TCK's Journey Through Cultural Transition*. Mumbai, India: Bottom Line Media, 2013.

O'Donnell, Kelly. *Global Member Care: The Pearls and Perils of Good Practice. Vol.* 1. Pasadena, CA: William Carey Library, 2011.

———. *Missionary Care: Counting the Cost for World Evangelization*. Pasadena, CA: William Carey Library, 1992.

Osiek, Carolyn. *Philippians, Philemon*. Abingdon New Testament Commentary. Nashville: Abingdon Press, 2000.

"Our Story." Upstream Collective. https://www.theupstreamcollective.org/our-story.

Peterson, David. *The Acts of the Apostles*. Pillar New Testament Commentary. Grand Rapids, MI: Eerdmans, 2009.

Piper, John. *Andrew Fuller: Holy Faith, Worthy Gospel, World Mission*. Wheaton, IL: Crossway, 2016.

Pirolo, Neal. "Four Levels of Missionary Care: Part One." Upstream Collective. 15 May 2019. https://www.upstreamcollective.org/post/four-levels-of-missionary-care-part-one.

————. "Four Levels of Missionary Care: Part Two." Upstream Collective. 15 May 2019. https://www.upstreamcollective.org/post/four-levels-of-missionary-care-part-two.

————. "Four Levels of Missionary Care: Part Three." Upstream Collective. 15 May 2019. https://www.upstreamcollective.org/post/four-levels-of-missionary-care-part-three.

————. *Serving as Senders Today*. Rev. ed. San Diego, CA: Emmaus Road International, Inc., 2012.

————. *The Reentry Team: Caring for Your Returning Missionaries*. San Diego, CA: Emmaus Road International, Inc., 2000.

Plummer, Robert L. and John Mark Terry. *Paul's Missionary Methods: In His Time and Ours*. Downers Grove, IL: InterVarsity Press, 2012.

Pollock, David C., Ruth E. Van Reken, and Michael V. Pollock. *Third Culture Kids: Growing Up Among Worlds*. 3rd ed. Boston, MA: Nicholas Brealey, 2017.

Pratt, Zane, M. David Sills, and Jeff K. Walters. *Introduction to Global Missions*. Nashville, TN: B&H Academic, 2014.

Ralston, Shirley. "Healthy at Home: Healthy Minds, Part One: Debriefing." Upstream Collective. 15 June 2021. https://www.upstreamcollective.org/post/healthy-at-home-healthy-minds-part-1-debriefing.

"ReMAP II: Worldwide Missionary Retention Study & Best Practices," World Evangelical Alliance. http://www.worldevangelicals.org/resources/rfiles/ res3_96_link_1292358945.pdf.

Scazzero, Peter. *Emotionally Healthy Spirituality: Unleash a Revolution in Your Life in Christ*. Grand Rapids, MI: Zondervan, 2006.

Schnabel, Eckhard J. Acts. ZECNT. Grand Rapids, MI: Zondervan, 2012.

————. *Paul the Missionary: The Realities, Strategies and Methods*. Downers Grove, IL: InterVarsity Press Academic, 2008.

Schreiner, Thomas R. *A Handbook on Acts and Paul's Letters*. Grand Rapids, MI: Baker Academic, 2019.

Sills, M. David. *Changing World, Unchanging Mission: Responding to Global Challenges*. Downers Grove, IL: InterVarsity Press, 2015.

————. *The Missionary Call: Find Your Place in God's Plan for the World*. Chicago, IL: Moody, 2008.

Silva, Moisés. *Philippians*. BECNT. 2nd ed. Grand Rapids, MI: Baker Academic, 1992, 2005.

Steffan, Tom and Lois McKinney Douglas. *Encountering Missionary Life and Work: Preparing for Intercultural Ministry*. Grand Rapids, MI: Baker Academic, 2008.

Stiles, Mack. "9 Marks of Healthy Missions." *9 Marks Journal: Missions* (Fall 2015): 31.

Storti, Craig. *The Art of Coming Home*. Boston, MA: Intercultural Press, 2003.

Stott, John R. W. *The Letters of John*. TNTC 19. Downers Grove, IL: InterVarsity Press Academic, 1988.

Terry, John Mark, ed. *Missiology: An Introduction to the Foundations, History, and Strategies of World Missions*. 2nd ed. Nashville, TN: B&H Academic, 2015.

Terry, John Mark and J. D. Payne. *Developing a Strategy for Missions: A Biblical, Historical, and Cultural Introduction*. Grand Rapids, MI: Baker Academic, 2013.

Turner, Jr., Gregg. "Are the Kids Alright? An Introduction to Missionary Kids and the Sending Church." Reaching & Teaching Blog. 19 January 2021. https://rtim.org/are-the-kids-alright/.

Voorwinde, Stephen. "More of Paul's Emotions in Philippians." *The Reformed Theological Review* 77, no. 1 (April 2018): 45–67.

Wilson, David J., ed. *Mind the Gaps: Engaging the Church in Missionary Care*. Colorado Springs, CO: Believers, 2015.

Wright, Eric E. *A Practical Theology of Missions: Dispelling the Mystery; Recovering the Passion*. Leominster, UK: Day One, 2018.

Yarbrough, Robert W. *1–3 John*. BECNT 15. Grand Rapids, MI: Baker Academic, 2008.

Young, Amy. *Looming Transitions: Starting and Finishing Well in Cross-Cultural Service*. Boston, MA: Amy Young, 2013.

Made in the USA
Columbia, SC
14 February 2023